VICTORIAN CRITICAL INTERVENTIONS

DETECTING THE NATION

Fictions of Detection and the Imperial Venture

CAROLINE REITZ

The Ohio State University Press
Columbus

Library of Congress Cataloging-in-Publication Data

Reitz, Caroline.
    Detecting the nation : fictions of detection and the imperial venture /
Caroline Reitz.
        p. cm. — (Victorian critical interventions)
    Includes bibliographical references and index.
        ISBN 0-8142-0982-3 (cloth : alk. paper) — ISBN 0-8142-5135-8
(pbk. : alk. paper) — ISBN 0-8142-9056-6 (cd-rom : alk. paper)
    1. Detective and mystery stories, English—History and criticism. 2.
English fiction—19th century—History and criticism. 3. Great Britain—
Colonies—In literature. 4. Imperialism in literature. 5. Colonies in litera-
ture. 6. Police in literature. I. Title. II. Series.
    PR830.D4R45 2004
    823'.087209358—dc22
                                            2004009551
    Cover design by Dan O'Dair
    Type set in Adobe Garamond
    Printed by Thomson-Shore, Inc.

The paper used in this publication meets the minimum requirements of
the American National Standard for Information Sciences—Permanence of
Paper for Printed Library Materials. ANSI Z39.48–1992.

9 8 7 6 5 4 3 2 1

For my parents, Bart and Ann Reitz, and
my husband, Doug Widmann

CONTENTS

SERIES EDITOR'S PREFACE

B oth Victorian studies and publishing in the field of Victorian studies are facing enormous challenges and opportunities in the twenty-first century. The field of Victorian studies today is not only multi- and interdisciplinary but also encompasses an ever widening variety of critical and theoretical interests, with no single methodology or theoretician predominating. Scholarly publishing too is changing dramatically as it begins to question traditional definitions of the "book" and to explore new and wider audiences for research-based publications. Reflecting these changes, *Victorian Critical Interventions* is a series of diverse, theory-based contributions to the broadly defined field of Victorian cultural studies, encompassing (but not limited to) literature and the arts, philosophy and religion, economics and empire, popular and political history, medicine and science, racial/sexual/gender identity, and even the text of "Victorian studies" itself. Uniquely, the series focuses on brief, accessibly written manuscripts that make brash and revisionary claims.

Until now, there has been no regular publication venue for works of critical analysis that need more than the space of a long article, but significantly less than that of a customary book. Indeed, nothing beyond professional convention defines a book as 250 or more printed pages. *Victorian Critical Interventions* provides a venue for publishing rigorously argued, scholarly books whose critical lenses are more sharply focused and whose arguments are more tightly constructed. Series entries also follow a specific, reader-friendly format: Each opens with an introduction that sets out the book's interventionist claims and surveys the context in which it is intervening, followed by three or four body chapters that cover its topic thoroughly, and then concludes with a clear, succinct assessment of the book's desired impact on the field of Victorian studies. Series entries are written to appeal to a diverse set of scholarly and student readers interested in clear delineations of the scholarly conversation on a particular topic, as well as one critic's attempt to reveal its omissions and add provocatively to it. Individually and as a group, series volumes work to redefine what we know and do as "Victorian studies" in the twenty-first century.

—Donald E. Hall

ACKNOWLEDGMENTS

T his book was written while moving almost as much as the Victorian detective: from Providence to Cambridge to New York to Cincinnati, and, finally, to St. Louis. And much like the detective, I needed the help of a large, sympathetic public to wrap up my investigations—and to remember where I lived. I must express my deepest thanks to Nancy Armstrong, who, as adviser of this work when it was a doctoral dissertation at Brown University, provided the perfect blend of insightful commentary, necessary skepticism, and good will. I can only hope, by way of thanks, to be the kind of rigorous, unflaggingly supportive adviser to my own students that Nancy has been to me. Bill Keach and Bob Scholes, from opposite ends of that long nineteenth century, added invaluable readings of my project at various stages. And from opposite ends of a sticky restaurant table, members of the Victorian Readers Group at Brown added important perspectives not only on this research but on the reasons for sticking with it: Lois Cucullu, Nick Daly, Julia Flanders, Ivan Kreilkamp, and Jennifer Ruth. I would like to thank many comrades at large, John Marx, Heather Hirschfeld, Carolyn Vellenga Berman, Tim Carens, and Kenneth Brewer, as well as the many readers of this manuscript, Ed Wiltse, Maire ni Fhlathuin, Kathy Psomiades, Daniel Cottom, and Julian Wolfreys. Donald E. Hall, the editor of The Ohio State University's Victorian Critical Interventions series, has been a model of encouragement and editorial speed. I thank him both for his attention to my manuscript and for the series. I would like to thank the press's anonymous readers for their many helpful suggestions, and the following editors at the press for their hard work and patience: Heather Lee Miller, Eugene O'Connor, and Leslie Evans.

I am thankful for the support and enthusiasm of my new colleagues here at Saint Louis University and in particular my chair, Sara van den Berg. I gratefully acknowledge the library staffs at Brown University, the New York Public Library, and Saint Louis University. Grants from Brown and Saint Louis University made possible the initial research and the polishing of the manuscript respectively. Finally I am grateful to the editors of the following journals for allowing permission to reprint previously published articles as revised portions of chapters 1 and 3:

"Bad Cop/Good Cop; Godwin, Mill, and the Imperial Origins of the English Detective." *Novel* 33, no. 2 (Spring 2000): 175–95. Copyright NOVEL Corp. ©2000. Reprinted with permission.

"Making an English Virtue of Necessity," *Genre* 31, nos. 3–4 (Fall/Winter 1998): 305–36. Reprinted with permission.

꒦꒷

While Sue Grafton and "Prime Suspect" might have had something to do with this book on the detective, it wouldn't be what it is and I wouldn't be who I am without the following very special teachers, who not only taught me how to read literature but, more importantly, showed me the relationship between literature and the larger world: Cynthia Briggs; Jeff Nunokawa; Nancy Armstrong, who read every word of this manuscript countless times; Bart Reitz, who thinks about literature from the vantage point of the larger world; and Nan Reitz, who has read every word of my writing since Carlos Brown was only a baby. My sister, Elizabeth Reitz Mullenix, is a role model in her work and in her life. It is one of my great joys to be in the same profession with her. My in-laws, Myra and Warren Widmann, have known me since before I was an English major, and I am thankful for their faith in a process which frequently seemed perverse even to me. Doug Widmann has been more supportive than words can express, spending many years in a crowded New York apartment watching me read and write and then spending a few more watching our sons so I could read and write. And finally, for those sons who seem to have inherited a maternal love of detective stories: Will, whose gimlet gaze misses less than Bucket, and Max, who is always in search of the third clue.

INTRODUCTION:
Imperial Detection

When Arthur Conan Doyle writes that Sherlock Holmes "takes my mind from better things," he is lamenting that Victorian England's most famous detective distracts him from writing in a more serious tradition: big historical novels that could bring the British Empire to life. Like Doyle, readers of detective fiction consider themselves distracted, though in their cases delightfully, from more serious fiction.[1] It is my contention that not only was detective fiction an important player in the arena of imperial literature, it both served and challenged the interests of Empire in a more direct way than either its status as fiction or the scholarship that declares it a minor genre wants to admit.[2] Criticism, particularly of detective fiction, has traditionally seen narratives of the domestic core and the imperial periphery in isolation from one another. As a result, two mysteries of Victorian national identity remain unsolved: (1) a shift over the course of the century from suspicion of to identification with the detective, and (2) a shift from insular lack of interest in to identification with the imperial project. Far from being a distraction from the grand motions of nineteenth-century history, nineteenth-century detective fiction, my study will demonstrate, helped a national readership imagine the British Empire in a way that was at once destabilizing and reassuring. The detective narrative turned national concerns about abuses of authority into a popular story about British authority in the contact zone of Victorian culture; this in turn allowed the detective and the imperial project to become extensions of rather than anathema to English national identity.

That the detective could serve as a representative of the British Empire—in Doyle's case a best selling representative—would have been impossible to imagine in the beginning of the nineteenth century, when the police and imperial expansion evoked profound suspicion from the English public.[3] Both were seen to require a level of aggression incompatible with national values of liberty and restraint. Reformers so diverse as Edmund Burke, William Godwin, and James Mill argued that no less than the fate of the nation required new stories about criminal justice and imperial expansion, stories that completely revised how the reading public saw these forms of government authority.[4] Detective fiction performed this revisionary work.

Over the course of a long nineteenth century, the detective narrative helped change public perception of domestic criminal justice and imperial expansion by producing a figure for the exercise of such power with whom English readers could identify. To succeed in this respect, the detective narrative had to reconcile the idea of individual liberty with the at times aggressive authority needed to maintain social order in a complex new imperial world. The modern detective was uniquely up to this task, I will argue, because his authority stemmed from knowledge rather than force and because this knowledge promised mastery of a specifically imperial world. As Thomas Richards has written, the fantasy of Empire is that it is "united not by force but by information" (1). The detective narrative provided a logical rationale for the precarious imperial project, which had to reconcile liberty with authority if the English public were to identify with the aims of imperial expansion.

Throughout the nineteenth century, as reformers established the boundaries of both the domestic crime problem and England's imperial authority, they invariably thought of one in terms of the other. As imperial expansion begot crime, the reasoning went, crime threatened the security and indeed the very character of Empire. As London's ports became host to an increasing number of ships bearing the goods of Empire, experts and intellectuals of various stripes argued that London was host to an increasing number of criminals, and this crisis inspired them to urge the British government to replace medieval systems of policing with a centralized and systematic force.[5] Contemporaneous debates about the transportation of criminals worked within the same domestic crime–imperial authority nexus. With the American Revolution preventing further transportation of convicts to America, England turned her sights to Australia and considered the opportunities that imperial expansion (in the form of a penal colony in New South Wales) provided for solving the domestic crime problem. Conversely, turn-of-the-century considerations of Empire focused on its criminal nature and made the same arguments for detection as criminal justice reformers.[6]

In reimagining detection as a modern and distinctly English methodology, the detective narrative promised a solution to the problem of excessive violence plaguing British authority at home and abroad. Whether starting from an argument about crime or from one about Empire, late-eighteenth- and early-nineteenth-century writers emphasized the problem of England's aggressive authority. From the sadistic crimes alleged in the Hastings trial, ground covered in chapter 1, to the naked aggression of Peterloo and the overly generous use of the scaffold, raw force appeared to be an uncomfortably frequent method of maintaining social control.[7] Nor was benign neglect an option for a forward looking nation; such a strategy would neither enable the acquisition and maintenance of territory on the peripheries nor ensure protection of the center.[8] The nation had to achieve a balance between the active authority necessary to maintain social order and the more restrained virtues valued by the English public. As reformers identified rules for the use of force at home and abroad, prevention of violence (explicitly criminal, implicitly governmental) quickly became the goal. Making prevention the first aim of government had two implications: (1) any government aggression could be represented as a response to violence and therefore defensive in nature, and (2) if English authority was to be distinguished by its defensive use of violence, a more proactive, everyday method of policing was necessary.[9] The detective story transformed archaic aggression into a more modern, benevolent authority by offering detection as the way of avoiding despotic displays of government authority.

By insisting that detective fiction offered readers participation in rather than a distraction from the grander tides of national history, my argument joins in the contemporary rethinking of the relationship between narrative and national identity—a relationship that will always be limited so long as we think of nations as distinct entities shaped from the inside out. Explicitly or not, such studies extend Benedict Anderson's crucial argument that print culture forges the "imagined community" of the nation, even as these studies also demonstrate that fiction challenges any sense of the nation as a distinct or homogeneous formation.[10] Traditional readings of detective fiction see the subgenre as particularly distinct and homogeneous. This understanding of the strict parameters of the detective story is as evident in such early considerations of the genre as Ronald Knox's ten commandments for the detective story ("A Detective Story Decalogue") and The Detection Club Oath's similar lists of *do*s and *don't*s, as it is in more contemporary treatments, such as John Cawelti's analysis of literary genres or D. A. Miller's considerations of it in *The Novel and the Police*.[11] I argue that this understanding of detective fiction has prevented our understanding the profound ways in which this fiction collaborated with other kinds of texts to shape national identity in Victorian England. I will be especially concerned to point out the continuities rather than the distinctions between the detective story and the colonial adventure story.

Before embarking on this argument, let me pause to specify what I mean by detective story. A good half of the texts I discuss are already classified as seminal works in the tradition of detective fiction: *Caleb Williams, Bleak House, The Moonstone,* and the Sherlock Holmes stories. And these texts do contain what we now recognize as the basic characteristics of a detective story: "a mysterious event or crime . . . at first concealing the solution from the reader but finally revealing it through the successful investigations of the detective."[12] While today we tend to identify the formal and thematic commonalties among these stories, I will venture the hypothesis that the authors were far more aware of where they overlapped with and differed from an entirely different body of texts. For most of the nineteenth century, what we now recognize as an English detective story pure and simple had not yet acquired its distinction as such, so compelling were its intersections and imbrications with other writing, especially the imperial adventure story.[13] The detective story entered into collaboration with and gave popular credence to such emerging discourses as institutional reform (of the criminal justice system or prisons, for example) and science (ethnography early in the century and criminology and anthropology later on). In addition, as I will contend throughout the book, the language and structure of such narratives as histories, political argument, travel writing, and journalism share so much with the detective narrative as to make distinguishing between such types of texts not impossible but far more problematic than has heretofore been recognized. Detective fiction was locked in a most intense and—I believe—mutually formative relationship with such narratives as histories of British India, English accounts of the Indian practice of Thuggee, and Kipling's imperial fiction. These narratives occupy an almost equally significant place in my argument.

I want to call attention to the relationship between the rise of domestic police power and the expansion of the British Empire—the twin stories at the heart of the detective narrative. But the relationships between these narratives are various. Sometimes the work of detection and imperial administration are drawn together by a larger ideology, which, for example, makes James Mill's account of the trial of Warren Hastings and Godwin's creation of protodetective Caleb Williams part of the same emerging narrative about the modern nation and its dependency on the power of local knowledge. The relationship may be one of resemblance, such as that between Wilkie Collins's characters Inspector Cuff, the detective, and Murthwaite, the explorer, in *The Moonstone.* At other times the relationship is genealogical, giving us the prototype for the modern detective celebrated by Dickens's midcentury journalism decades earlier in the colonial administrators who become the Thug Police.

If the continuities between the detective who detects crime and the explorer who performs the work of imperial administration are indeed more com-

pelling than scholarship has been willing to acknowledge, then we must ultimately question the critical-theoretical tendency to imagine the nation as a
domestic core that was purely English and a colonial periphery that was foreign and racially marked. This tendency is itself a version of a Victorian self-
fashioning that prevented the reader from acknowledging the manifold
interdependencies between the two domains. Making a distinction between
the epistemologies of domestic policing and imperial administration enabled
a reassuring compartmentalization of what was in actuality threateningly
interdependent. And so we continue to read detective fiction as a modern conception of the metropolitan center, personified and policed by Sherlock
Holmes, and imperial fiction as an exotic rendering of the colonial periphery,
personified and policed by Kim's Kimball O'Hara. This tradition of scholarship reads only that part of the detective story that shows the detective gradually becoming a familiar part of the English literary landscape and neglects
to consider why this happens to be so: why, that is, the detective can become
more English only as the world he patrols becomes increasingly foreign.[14]
Thus Dickens's detectives become easier to imagine as one of "us" as Dickens's
London is invaded by foreigners visiting the Great Exhibition or as the city
becomes an almost unrecognizable wilderness to Mr. Snagsby, a lifelong
London resident, in *Bleak House.* I propose to consider both fictions of detection and imperial narratives as mutually informing participants in a cultural
project that by the time of Doyle and Kipling would be called the Great
Game. To ignore this fact, as I have just suggested, is to reproduce a now-out-
dated fantasy of Victorian national identity, which imagined, according to
Simon Gikandi, "that the connections between metropolitan center and its
colonial periphery were loose and ephemeral, that the character of the island
nation remained unaltered by its long and extensive contact with colonial
spaces" (78). Mary Louise Pratt has famously described the "contact zone"
generated by colonial encounter as a contested imperial space. While it means
literally a colonial frontier, she defines a "contact" perspective as "that which
emphasizes how subjects are constituted in and by their relations to each
other. It treats the relations among colonizers and colonized . . . not in terms
of separateness or apartheid, but in terms of copresence, interaction, inter-
locking understandings and practices, often within radically asymmetrical
relations of power" (7). The mutual dependency of domestic and imperial narratives, such as the detective story and the colonial adventure story, provides
a model of how Victorian culture became just such a contact zone, as it spread
and incorporated other cultures.

Broadly speaking, this challenge requires me to show that such binary distinctions as center/periphery—like those that distinguish men from women,

normal from abnormal, or nature from culture—are the result of various cultural practices of classification. Because this argument is fundamentally about identity—that of cultural figures, readers, nations, and genres—I am situating my claims in the wider theoretical context of identity formation. My argument that two genres associated with seemingly distinct geographical and narrative spaces are in fact mutually informing aspects of the same project draws on the critical traditions of Michel Foucault on the one hand and Deconstruction on the other. To claim that Foucault and Deconstruction are headwaters of a single critical river is no doubt objectionable for reasons too numerous to go into here. My aim is not to ignore the different practices and problems of critics working with these theories, but rather to draw on what I see to be a shared interest in the paradoxical nature of identity formation. Critics ranging from Peter Stallybrass and Allon White to Judith Butler, Barbara Johnson, Edward Said, Gayatri Chakravorty Spivak, and V. Y. Mudimbe turn the question of difference into a set of procedures that demonstrate how identity is formed on the basis of difference, whether difference of social position, gender, sexuality, race, or nationality.[15] These critics ask us to consider that while we need such concrete identity categories in order to imagine ourselves and our nation, these categories are not based on some truth—be it subject or object—prior to culture. These categories themselves—both those to which we belong and those to which we cannot belong and still be who we are—endow human beings with our most essential characteristics (gender or race, for example). Being almost foundationless, such categories are most unstable precisely when they appear to be the most concrete, when, as in the cases of gender or race, they appear to be features of the body itself. Stallybrass and White show how cultures achieve the appearance of internal coherence and continuity in time as they "think themselves" through oppositions: "The high/low opposition is a fundamental basis [of] . . . sense-making in European cultures" (3). In her work on gender identity, Butler similarly argues that such oppositions are necessary for "cultural intelligibility" (17). But even though, as she says, identity can only be consolidated in "the act of differentiating the two oppositional moments of the binary" (23), that does not mean that identity of any kind thereby achieves stability. In order to perform the foundational act of differentiation that gives an individual or nation its distinctive character as such, that individual or nation must incorporate precisely what it will henceforth locate outside as the external limit of itself: "each extremity structures the other, depends upon and invades the other in certain historical moments" (Stallybrass and White 3–4).

According to this tradition of thinking, such categories of identity are consequently governed by a chiasmatic logic that defines two terms in opposition to one another. To do so, this logic incorporates each term in its opposite and then expels it to define each term by virtue of its not being the other. As Johnson explains, "each is already inhabited by the other as a difference from itself" (35). Mudimbe's work is especially helpful in bringing this logic to bear on the colonialist project.[16] To show that "colonializing structures" are particularly given to producing a "dichotomizing system," he explains how the chiasmus of identity formation operates in a colonial situation: "The African has become not only the Other who is everyone except me, but rather the key which, in its abnormal differences, specifies the identity of the Same" (12). The fantasy of a clear distinction promised by such a dichotomy is continually broken down. As Ian Baucom explains, the Empire "is the place onto which the island kingdom arrogantly displaces itself and from which a puzzled England returns as a stranger to itself" (3).[17]

I will follow this logic as it unfolds historically in relation both to a Victorian national identity predicated upon an opposition between center and margin and to the formulation of "opposing" literary categories—detective fiction and imperial adventure narratives—which have shaped and continue to shape our understanding both of that national identity and of the role that literature plays in shaping it. The notion of identity as the product of the construction and deconstruction of oppositional categories is central to my work here as I consider how something marginal—the foreign figure of the turn-of-the -century detective—gets repositioned at the core of modern metropolitan society. Grasping the chiasmatic logic of identity formation offers a way of addressing these questions:

How did the police, specifically called "not English" at the moment of their creation in 1829, become English?[18]

How did English acceptance of the police provide a vehicle for the acceptance of the then equally suspect imperial project?

How does identification on the part of the English public with both the police and the Empire demonstrate how that which is marginal becomes the key to specifying the identity of the center?

Criticism traditionally sees detective fiction as offering comforting resolutions to such questions, partly because these accounts tend to validate rather than challenge traditional accounts of the rise of the police or the rise of Empire.[19] Thus, we are encouraged to read the detective narrative in allegorical relation to Whig historians' accounts of the homegrown emanation of the police from English values.[20] I will focus instead on the confusing omnipresence of an imperial narrative within the detective story. The peaceful order of England, for example, is confounded by Empire in what T. S. Eliot called the "first and greatest of English detective novels": Collins's *The Moonstone*. As the novel's main narrator, Gabriel Betteredge, complains, "here was our quiet English house suddenly invaded by a devilish Indian Diamond" (36). The diamond leaves the house, but never the novel; a detective figure tracking it to the wilds of India literally has the last word. Similarly, Doyle's *The Sign of the Four* cannot tell a story of English crime without placing an account of the Indian Mutiny at its center.

While the mutually defining relationship of center and periphery is a now-standard observation in Postcolonial Studies, Victorian Studies, in particular scholarly work on detective fiction, has been more reluctant to take the principle to heart.[21] This tendency has been aggravated by the influence of *Discipline and Punish*, Michel Foucault's account of the role of surveillance in modern formations of power, particularly his theory of panopticism, as well as an enormously influential application of that theory in D. A. Miller's *The Novel and the Police*. Lauren M. E. Goodlad has recently called on scholars working in Victorian Studies to "modify Foucault's analysis" (2003, 545). Goodlad makes a very sensible argument that as *Discipline and Punish* is not about Victorian Britain—with the exception of the Panopticon, Foucault's focus is on French history—it cannot be an accurate lens through which to look at the Victorian past.[22] Her point is not that the manifest interest Victorian Studies has in Foucault is limiting, but rather that we have been interested in only a limited Foucault. Goodlad steers scholars toward Foucault's later works on "governmentality" with good reason. But my point here is that we need, particularly in the wake of Miller's persuasive placement of the "police" at the heart of the Victorian novel, to take a closer look at panopticism and how the rise of the detective in Victorian literature and culture questions principles central to these powerful readings.

THE BLINDSPOTS OF PANOPTICISM

"Panopticism" is, by definition, a hard idea to resist. Foucault characterizes it as "an indefinitely generalizable mechanism" (216). In his discussion of panopticism as a disciplinary mechanism, Foucault is certainly not concerned with detective fiction;[23] neither is it Miller's central focus. While the novels Miller considers feature detectives and detective work, he is more interested in the police as a theme and a strategy: "This work centers not on the police, in the modern institutional shape they acquire in Western liberal culture during the nineteenth century, but on the ramification within the same culture of less visible, less visibly violent modes of 'social control'" (viii). Indeed, a major part of Miller's argument is that the actual police, as characters in the novels, are limited and confined as the power they stand for becomes more generalized in an increasingly carceral culture. But Foucault's and Miller's readings of discipline in nineteenth-century culture and literature have helped cast the image of the detective and the discipline he would seem to embody as a sure-footed symbol of an always already policed world. I remain persuaded by both *Discipline and Punish* and *The Novel and the Police* that surveillance has as much power as raw force in modern culture; there is much evidence across the vast array of Victorian writing to support Foucault's argument that the history of the nineteenth century shows a shift from "violent forms of power" toward a multiplicity of "subtle, calculated technolog[ies] of subjection" (221). Certainly, my argument about a gradual public acceptance of and identification with the police is greatly indebted to Foucault's representation of how a society becomes disciplined; the nineteenth-century detective, who acquires his cultural authority through knowledge rather than force, owes much to Foucault's equation of knowledge and power; and, finally, my argument that the detective is a figure whose authority needs to be read as operating both at home and in the far reaches of the British Empire requires that power be "generalizable." But there are two chief problems in applying the work of Foucault and Miller to both the literary and cultural figures of the detective and, moreover, to the operations of power in a colonial context: (1) the representation of power as opposing itself to "mixture," and (2) a representation of knowledge as a complete body or, to use Thomas Richards's term, "comprehensive."[24]

Foucault begins his chapter on panopticism with a fascinating discussion of the plague and how society responded to the threat by enclosing individuals in their houses and subjecting them to unprecedented investigation: "Against the plague, which is a mixture, discipline brings into play its power, which is one of analysis" (197). Along the same lines, Foucault later suggests that "one of the primary objects of discipline is to fix; it is an anti-nomadic technique. . . . It arrests or regulates movements; it clears up confusion" (218–19). Through investigation, then, discipline works to separate, contain, and fix, hence the appeal of architecture: Bentham's idea of the Panopticon. What this powerful argument does not take into account, perhaps cannot take into account, is the historical specificity of the English detective. As I argue in the following chapters, the English detective, seemingly an ideal agent of a disciplinary regime of investigation and analysis, is himself a mixture, a site of profound cultural struggle over the meaning of English authority. From early suspicions about the English detective that he was a Frenchified spy hostile to the values of liberal culture to lingering concerns over the quasi-military nature of such a force (English society is still debating whether bobbies should carry arms), the contested or "contact" figure of the English detective was always straddling the very binaries that Foucault has discipline policing: "mad/sane; dangerous/harmless; normal/abnormal" (199). As Miller explains, "discipline is interested in putting in place a perceptual grid in which a division between the normal and the deviant inherently imposes itself" (18).

The detective would seem to embody the Foucaultian equation of knowledge and power in which, from the eighteenth century on, "the formation of knowledge and the increase of power regularly reinforce one another in a circular process" (224).[25] But Foucault's representation of knowledge is too general in *Discipline and Punish*. While Foucault's representation of power is mobile, always circulating, it does so in order to form "a body of knowledge" (220). While knowledge is partial—indeed Foucault is famously interested in "the infinitely small of political power" (214), "the infinitesimal level of individual lives" (222)—it ultimately hangs together in an "infinitely minute web" (224). In "order to be exercised," Foucault explains, "this power had to be given the instrument of permanent, exhaustive, omnipresent surveillance, capable of making all visible" (214). Knowledge is always ultimately centralizable. The Panopticon's central tower is never too far away.

One of the things that this influential representation of knowledge does, Erin O'Connor has recently argued, is "to conflate knowing with containing, classifying, and controlling" (242). In his discussion of *Oliver Twist*, Miller writes that "the story of the Novel is essentially the story of an active regulation" (10). Too often the figure of the nineteenth-century detective is that of the Panopticon's central tower with legs. Some recent critical work does consider the larger social context in which the detective story emerges. Nevertheless, these critics, writing in the wake of *The Novel and the Police*, still provide a too-tidy explanation of the rise of the detective figure in which both imperial and police power are almost effortlessly panoptical, and the detective the embodiment of this power.[26] Ronald R. Thomas calls *Bleak House*'s Bucket a "benevolent panoptical machine" (1997, 135). But it was my perception, when first reading these texts years ago, that all of this knowledge gathering done by detectives and imperial explorers was as threatening to the idea of control as it was a demonstration of control. One only has to think of Bucket thrown temporarily but fatally off the track by Lady Dedlock's disguise or Cuff's initial incorrect suspicion of Rachel in *The Moonstone*, or of Dickens's celebrated detectives having their pockets picked on the way home from the Household Words offices to understand that the knowledge/power of the detective is partial. The red herrings and false accusations of fictions of detection suggest that knowledge, as Richards explains, "ran off in many directions like the hedgehogs in Alice's game of croquet" (4). The idea of a comprehensive knowledge is always compromised, if also abetted, by its local quality.

In all manner of discourse, from courtroom speeches to colonial treatises to works of fiction, detection was represented as the acquisition and centralization of "local knowledge," a ubiquitous phrase in these texts. Local knowledge was the product of rigorous observation aided by familiarity with the people and circumstances observed. Familiarity bred not contempt so much as understanding, which had the advantage of being a nonviolent form of crime prevention.[27] But while representing policing as knowledge gathering seemed to solve the problem of excessive violence for the Victorians, the emphasis on knowledge troubled the consolidation of imperial authority in ways that challenge the terms in which we understand Victorian epistemology. The British Empire was built on the imperial gaze as embodied by Bentham's Panopticon, the British survey of the Indian subcontinent, and all the visual technologies that remade the Empire a single world in miniature. At the same time, Victorian knowledge like Victorian realism was based on an accumulation of details, any of which might be either essential or inconsequential. These epistemologies, paradigmatic and local, or comprehensive and positive, were far more dependent on one another than cultural theory has heretofore been willing to acknowledge. Local knowledge allowed propolice reformers—in England and India—to win public favor for the centralized authority necessary for effective policing. Samuel Smiles's article titled "The Police of London" explains that policemen were directed "to make themselves roughly acquainted with the geography of their respective sections . . . the police-constable is even expected to possess such a knowledge of the inhabitants of each house as to enable him to recognize their persons" (101). On the one hand, this description made centralized authority seem reassuringly English. Indeed, Smiles goes on to explain that the constable needed to recognize people in order "to render assistance when he is called upon to do so." At the same time, this article paradoxically suggests that first-hand information was somehow truer knowledge than that which was administered if not gathered from afar. My own argument attempts to return a sense of this paradox to the figure of the detective, to return him to the contact zone from which he has been removed.

Putting the detective in the contact zone, however, does not necessarily keep us from the problem of panopticism. So generalizable is the theory of panopticism that it has been almost equally attractive to critics of imperial literature as to those of detective fiction. While I will explore this tendency in more detail in subsequent chapters, such as in recent treatments of the phenomenon of

Thuggee or of Kipling's writing, it is important here to note the relationship between some of the foundational work of Colonial/Postcolonial Studies and Foucault's characterizations of discipline. "I have found it useful here to employ Michel Foucault," Said writes in his ground-breaking *Orientalism*. Drawing in part on *Discipline and Punish,* Said explains that "without examining Orientalism as a discourse one cannot possibly understand the enormously systematic discipline by which European culture was able to manage—and even produce—the Orient politically, sociologically, militarily, ideologically, scientifically, and imaginatively during the post-Enlightenment period" (3). What happens when the theory of panopticism travels to a colonial context is that the center watchtower becomes the metropolitan center and the penitentiary's periphery becomes the native population. Panoptic discipline becomes a model of us versus them. We see this in Said's subsequent description of Victorian writing, which, he notes, is indebted to Foucault's ideas in *Discipline and Punish:*

> For every idea about 'our' art spoke for by Arnold, Ruskin, Mill, Newman, Carlyle, Renan, Gobineau, or Comte, another link in the chain binding 'us' together was formed while another outsider was banished. Even if this is always the result of such rhetoric, wherever and whenever it occurs, we must remember that for nineteenth-century Europe an imposing edifice of learning and culture was built, so to speak, in the face of actual outsiders (the colonies, the poor, the delinquent), whose role in the culture was to give definition to what they were constitutionally unsuited for (1993, 228).

A colonial context amplifies the paradox at the heart of panopticism: "One sees everything," Foucault explains, "without ever being seen" (202). Scholars, such as Timothy Mitchell, have applied Foucault's formulation to the imperial scene. Mitchell discusses the point of view of a European observer in the Middle East: "the point of view was not just a place set apart, outside the world or above it. Ideally, it was a position from where, like the authorities in Bentham's panopticon, one could see and yet not be seen" (306). But Mitchell goes on to recognize the paradox of such a subject position: "There was a contradiction . . . between the need to separate oneself from the world and render it up as an object of representation, and the desire to lose oneself within this object-world and experience it directly" (307). This paradox is even more pronounced for the detective or colonial administrator who is having an official rather than—or in addition to—an aesthetic experience. The distance implied by panopticism's invisibility must be continually broken down by the detective's constant forays into the unstable domain of the local. In short, contrary to the logic of the Panopticon, the power of sur-

veillance supplies a vital link between center and periphery as much as it rei-
fies a difference between them. By tracking the power of surveillance as it
emerges in the form of the detective, I intend to challenge the "us–them"
model of panopticism presently associated with imperial authority, Victorian
national identity, and the figure of the detective. Like the opposition of
us–them, literary criticism, by opposing detective stories to imperial narratives, replays the Victorian hope that the detective will do the work of
England and not the work of Empire, so that the two—England and her
Empire—can remain separate and distinct. But even as these detective narratives at times gratify our taxonomic fantasy, they never fail to reveal the
murky relation between island nation and sprawling empire that such a fantasy presupposes. They record in fact how central is a knowledge of the imperial world to the work of the New Police and how it is the involvement in this
new imperial world that, paradoxically, is the detective's ticket home to
English respectability. In making an English virtue of an imperial necessity,
detective fiction not only set off a shift in national identification with both
the detective and the imperial project, but also refashioned Englishness as an
imperial instead of an insular identity. Itself a product of heated debates
about national character, detective fiction made that which was beyond
England's borders essential to defining what was within.

To demonstrate how the detective narrative shaped this complex new
imperial reality for a Victorian readership, my chapters focus for the most part
on writers traditionally understood to represent, if not diametrically opposed
positions in the debate about English authority, then at least significantly different ones: Godwin and Mill; Dickens and Wilkie Collins; and Kipling and
Doyle. Because the detective narrative works to provide a story sufficiently
coherent as to enable the English reader's identification with the detective, my
readings will stress the foundational assumptions concerning identity in general and English identity in particular on which these opposing camps must
agree in order to disagree with one another. My point is to show that the
necessity for the detective was the end result of at least two very different lines
of argumentation. Like the national identity he came to embody, the figure
of the modern detective came into being as the means of reconciling contesting opinions about English authority.[28] The critical division of labor that
would make them opposed, rather than mutually dependent, forms of writing, like the distinction between center and periphery itself, only preserves the
production of Victorian nationalism as an unsolved mystery. The following
chapters strive to reverse that literary-historical tendency.

ᴤ 1 ᴤ

BAD COP/GOOD COP:
Godwin, Mill, and the Imperial Origins of the English Detective

O
ur understanding of detective fiction as a strictly domestic genre takes its cue from the standard line of histories of the English police: English police embody, from their albeit contested beginning, national values such as mild justice and local autonomy, as opposed to the centralized authority of foreign models of policing, such as that of France.[1] T. A. Critchley, a twentieth-century historian of the police, provides an exemplary description of such a position: the "character" of England's "mild system of police . . . owe[s] everything to native manners, nothing at all to foreign influences" (55). Such a story forgets the police's imperial origins in the early and formative police systems in Ireland and India, thereby enabling the police to be read as a homegrown invention.[2] The view that the detective genre "owes everything to native manners" has become the standard history of the detective genre, as well. And *Caleb Williams,* with its searing criticism of and resolution in the English criminal justice system, is seen by critics to inaugurate this insular genre.[3]

What Godwin's novel demonstrates, however, is precisely the opposite: (1) that the detective genre emerges from debates about the global crisis of English authority, and (2) that the way of coping with the domestic disruption posed by the rise of an organized police force was paradoxically to explore the character of English authority in the colonies. Godwin's detective narrative is a product of contemporary social criticism that sought to connect rather than distinguish between the crimes of English law at home and abroad. Godwin sought to tell a new story of English criminal justice by writing about colonial governance. Reading Godwin's novel, originally titled

1

Things as They Are; or, The Adventures of Caleb Williams, in the context of his contemporaneous writings on Empire invites an examination of another turn-of-the-century exploration of "things as . . . they really are," James Mill's *The History of British India,* in the context of an emerging discourse about detective work and the rise of the police (5:405).[4] If Godwin shapes a genre out of the reform debates of this period, Mill's history creates a new genre of civil servant—one who detects and solves crimes—out of these same debates. Together these texts produce, in the words of Mill, the "enlightened inquirer" as the good cop versus the bad cop of the arbitrary and despotic power of the late-eighteenth-century state. In order to do so, both Godwin and Mill use the colonies to imagine a new—and newly acceptable—kind of English authority. This authority figure would be taken up by their fellow reformers in their hard sell of the police to, at that time, a passionately skeptical English public.

In the strange brew of early-nineteenth-century reform (one that would find Godwin and Mill as often in opposition as agreement), *Caleb Williams* (1794) and *The History of British India* (1817) provided both a logic and a discourse for emerging propolice arguments, such as George B. Mainwaring's *Observations on the Present State of the Police of the Metropolis* (1821) and John Wade's *A Treatise on the Police and Crimes of the Metropolis* (1829), that the detective, far from undermining English values, could embody benevolent, modern knowledge in the imperial nation's service. The four sections of this chapter attempt to show the evolution of this argument: The first briefly covers the strange alliances of reformers in debates over the character of English justice abroad; the second argues for the necessity of reading Godwin's contributions to the detective genre and the figure of the English detective in the context of Empire; the third explores Mill's refinement of detection as a solution for the mismanagement of British India; and the concluding section traces the influence that Godwin's and Mill's writings had on arguments made by propolice reformers in the first decades of the nineteenth century.

Strange Bedfellows

Godwin's and Mill's writings were part of a vigorous debate about the crisis of a criminal justice system that, reformers argued, had itself become criminal in both its domestic and imperial applications. The final decades of the eighteenth century saw the trial of Warren Hastings, Governor General of India, the breakdown of the Bloody Code, the development of the transportation system to Australia, Pitt's suspension of *habeas corpus,* the use of

informers, and the arrests and state trials of political radicals. The legal system became "a recurring target of radical polemic" and the despotic un-
English character of *the* English institution, the law, a subject of passionate
concern (Ignatieff 160).

Debates over the criminal character of English law at home and abroad
made strange bedfellows and generated the paradoxical logic that what was
wrong with England was most apparent by looking outside it. In his seven-year
prosecution of Warren Hastings, Edmund Burke focused on the need for
national recognition of English criminal activity overseas.[5] Reformers of
almost every stripe, from Bentham and Mill to Godwin, who reviled (and
were reviled by) Burke after his apparent change of heart over the French
Revolution, celebrated the liberty-loving spirit of his prosecution of Hastings.[6]
Indeed an increasingly widespread concern that English law, the ostensible
cornerstone of liberty, was really a vehicle for despotism gave rise to a diverse
reform movement; as E. P. Thompson suggests, "'Radicalism' came to include
very diverse tendencies as the 19th century advanced" (1966, 466). Turn-of-
the-century radicalism united the two very diverse subjects of this chapter:
Godwin, the utopian anarchist, and James Mill, advocate of "good government" and representative of the authoritarian strain in Utilitarianism.[7]
According to John Plamenatz, Mill's "radical utilitarianism. . . . repudiated
nothing more vigorously" than the Godwinian beliefs of "anarchism and com-
munism" (97). While Godwin and Mill represent an apparent paradox
between liberty and authority in turn-of-the-century reform, what these very
different men share in their capacities as "radicals," in addition to numerous
mutually influential acquaintances,[8] is the imperial context of their critiques of
English criminal justice—most evident in their attacks on Warren Hastings
and his brand of imperial authority.

Godwin and Mill both wrote with Burkean extravagance about the actions
of Hastings and their disastrous effects on English national character. In letters to William Pitt, published in *The Political Herald* during Parliamentary
debates over Hastings's possible impeachment, Godwin characterizes
Hastings as "a despotic and imperious veteran," the head of a "memorable
band of East Indian culprits." "Whatever of humanity remained to us,"
Godwin continues, "started with horror from the caprices of tyranny and the
oppressions of avarice in that quarter of the world" (Marken and Pollin 22,
24, 31). In the lengthy account of the trial in *The History of British India* that,
arguably, became the dominant reading of the Hastings affair through the
twentieth century, Mill suggests that even the notoriously excessive Burke did
not go far enough in his analysis of what the iniquities of the Hastings administration represented (5:200–201). The similar responses of Godwin and Mill

to Hastings's "high crimes and misdemeanors" not only register their larger concerns about England's precarious claims to civilization but also demonstrate their very similar solution as well: detection.

Both Godwin and Mill argued in the aftermath of Hastings that the legitimacy of English civilization both at home and overseas could only be restored if the public were guided by "a spirit of investigation" (Godwin 1985, 82), a "homebred understanding" (Godwin 1985, 552) embodied in an "enlightened inquirer" (Mill 6:7) who could "detect the artifices" of "mysterious" government (Godwin 1985, 552) and perform the "investigation of . . . those complicated scenes of action" (Mill 1:xxv) that imperiled the English virtues of reason and truth, justice and benevolence. While *Caleb Williams* is recognized as a founding text of the English detective genre, as well as a narrativization of contemporary domestic political debates, that same tradition has ignored the novel's relationship to Godwin's intervention in the debate about English law overseas. This oversight has enormous implications for the way we understand the history of the genre. Indeed, why, given the stress on the formal and domestic origins of detective fiction, should *The History of British India* be seen as a component of an emerging detective genre; John Kenneth Galbraith quips in his introduction to the 1968 edition that Mill's *History* hasn't been read at all since its days as a handbook for Company servants. Together, I nevertheless want to argue, these texts reimagined the detective in the age of the bad cop—the age of Peterloo and government spies—as necessary for the progress of an expanding nation. The good cop authored by Godwin and Mill came to articulate an imperial logic that they did not live long enough to see.[9]

Caleb Williams AND IMPERIAL AUTHORITY

Godwin's writings in the 1780s on crises in the British Empire provide as crucial a context for *Caleb Williams* as critics have argued about *Political Justice*.[10] These writings provide a rough draft of the argument that Godwin will make to a larger audience, he hopes, by turning to fiction in *Caleb Williams:* What is wrong with England is a *criminal* justice system at home and abroad that needs a modern spirit of investigation to set it right.[11] In the process of converting arguments about Empire to a novel about England, Godwin turns a critique of imperial authority into an argument for a new type of local hero.

As an active participant in the broad range of reform debates at the end of the eighteenth century, Godwin's knowledge of the central texts of criminal legal reform has been well documented. He knew well John Howard's condemnatory surveys of British prisons, citing him in *Caleb Williams* as his source for the descriptive passages about Caleb's incarceration.[12] Godwin's familiarity with the *Newgate Calendar* and the *State Trials* also figures in the novel. The fugitive Caleb, making a living as an anonymous writer, turns to "histories of celebrated robbers . . . and other memorable worthies, whose career[s were] terminated upon the gallows or the scaffold" (268). Caleb himself is the celebrated subject of a handbill, authored and distributed by Gines under the auspices of Falkland, that pursues him in his peripatetic evasion of persecution.

Less well documented is the relationship between this early and influential detective novel and Godwin's writings on imperial criminality, which consist of the letters of "Mucius" in *The Political Herald* and the incomplete "Memoirs of the Administration of the Government of Madras during the Presidency of Lord McCartney" in the same journal, ground covered by Mill's fifth and most powerful volume of *The History*. Godwin writes of Burke's efforts against Hastings:

> Having exerted every faculty and every excellence within the circle of the human mind, he closes this long and splendid career with a great public prosecution, the example of which may wash away the stains of Britain, and ensure security and peace to generations yet unborn. (20)

According to Godwin, the Hastings prosecution highlighted Burke's brilliance and England's benevolence. In a letter to Dundas, then treasurer of the Navy, Godwin argues "the accusation of Mr. Hastings continues to appear to me not inferior in importance to any business that was ever brought before a British parliament" (36). Far from chiming in with contemporary criticism of the protracted nature of the impeachment trial, Godwin explains that he will indeed try and add to the "length into which the business must inevitably run": "It shall be my business, in my humble sphere, to endeavour to keep alive the attention of the public by such hints, animadversions and reflections, as a business so various in its tenour, and comprehensive in its subject, cannot fail to suggest". (36)

From the "humble sphere" of the impecunious political hack (*The Political Herald* would run out of financial steam shortly thereafter), Godwin gave his version of English crimes abroad. Hastings's Company cronies are "devouring locusts," who, in accordance with "the practice of the servants of the British government in this quarter of the world . . . grasp at the largest sums" (67, 95). The "despotic and imperious" Hastings embodies not only this greed, but a worse crime, one more antithetical to the noble, albeit bedraggled, spirit of English civilization: obstruction of justice. Much as Mill would later argue,

Godwin explains that Hastings's primary crime is the use of his influence to obfuscate investigation into the things as they are in India. Godwin speaks here as "an Englishman" concerned with the "baleful infection" of the "East Indian culprits." The unseen danger metaphorically implied in "infection" will "root away the last remains of British honour and British virtue" (24).

Suggesting a dangerous parallel between the British and the Roman empires, Godwin argues that a lack of honest judicial inquiry was responsible for the "miserable and degenerate" "affairs at Rome." The British Empire needs a Cicero to "openly and fearlessly [state] to the public the cause of this miscarriage" (37). A bold spirit of investigation is necessary, Godwin implies, to keep London from going the way of Rome. Godwin continued this theme in his "Memoirs" written in the same years, 1785–1786, as the Mucius letters. Though the "Memoirs" would be left unfinished because *The Political Herald* folded, Godwin's argument was clear: Curiosity can restore the British character, which has been damaged by the confounding of innocence and guilt. "There seems to be a spirit too general in this country," Godwin writes, "of confounding the virtue and the vice, the right and wrong of the persons who have been concerned in the direction of our affairs in India" (62). In a passage that underscores the risk posed to national character by crime overseas, Godwin argues that the solution to this problem is English curiosity:

> The curiosity of the public can scarcely take a more useful direction; and we are delirious both to indulge and to assist it. The character and the prosperity of this country are both of them inseparably involved in the business of India. It is impossible that every man of benevolence and philanthropy should not be anxious for the first of these. That cruelty, tyranny, usurpation and avarice should be considered as constituting the character of Britain in any part of the world, he will sincerely lament. (61)

In *Caleb Williams,* published the year before Hastings's acquittal, with its intensely *curious* hero who muses that "innocence and guilt are too much confounded in human life" (122), Godwin at last completes his unfinished Empire writings—and finds his Cicero.

Caleb Williams is littered with the "structure of attitude and reference" toward Empire that Edward Said argues is part of the culture of imperialism. At least part of Falkland's fortune comes from West Indian property, the business of which holds at bay Caleb's one possible ally, Collins. Godwin draws numerous comparisons between Caleb's persecution and those peoples oppressed around the globe: the Jew, the "West Indian negro," "a Cherokee chieftain at the falls of the Mississippi" (149, 273). Falkland's fanatical concern with his reputation, which fuels his hatred for Caleb, has clear imperialist implications: "My character shall be revered as spotless and unimpeachable by all posterity, as long as the name of Falkland shall be repeated in the most distant regions of the many-peopled globe" (292). Falkland's identification with imperialist rapacity becomes even clearer in the debate at the literal and symbolic center of this text where Falkland defends Alexander in the face of Caleb's critique of imperial conquest. When the cheeky Caleb wonders "if murder and massacre were but a very left-handed way of producing civilisation and love," Falkland replies that Alexander "has been much misunderstood" (116–17). "It was necessary to the realising of his project," Caleb's master explains, "that he should pass for a god" (117). In case the reader somehow missed this connection, Godwin has Caleb wonder at the end of the novel:

> When Nero and Caligula swayed the Roman sceptre, it was a fearful thing to offend these bloody rulers . . . Falkland! art thou the offspring, in whom the lineaments of these tyrants are faithfully preserved? Was the world, with all its climates, made in vain for thy helpless, unoffending victim?. (324)

One of the first English detective novels, then, literally centers on a problem that had long been on Godwin's mind: the rotten character of imperial authority.

Godwin's savage critique in *Caleb Williams* of "the law" that has "neither eyes, nor ears, nor bowels of humanity . . . and turns into marble the hearts of all those that are nursed in its principles" (288) is familiar critical terrain. As the novel's full title says, it is a look at "things as they are" in the final decade of the eighteenth century and, as critics have amply shown, Godwin found things wanting. The focus of my argument, though, is on how this critique of the contemporary legal system articulates a sense of things as they could be—given an individual capable of making that system work for rather than against the English people. Caleb is Godwin's attempt to create this New Man. Donald Harvey explains that "Caleb's claims to represent the *new* is merely implied—sufficiently clearly . . . in view of his numerous criticisms of society—but implied nonetheless" (245). However, arguing that Caleb is a protodetective on the beat of imperial trespasses against the British character, and therefore associated with the "new," goes against traditional readings of the meaning of Caleb's detective work. These critics have Godwin, like most of his fellow Englishmen and all of his fellow radicals, lambasting the system of government spies and informers, of which Caleb is just an amateur version.

Ian Ousby makes the most comprehensive argument that Godwin is critical of Caleb and that "the criticism of Caleb the detective and the hostility to the spy draw their life from the same ground" (31). Ousby explains that "Caleb's detection involves a disregard for those basic qualities—sincerity and sensitivity—upon which Godwin's ideal social code was based" (37).

It is true that Godwin detested spies. He criticizes the "most crying evil" of "spies and informers" in a 1793 letter to the *Morning Chronicle* on free speech (Marken and Pollin 113). Falkland's lackey Gines, like most people in late-eighteenth-century law enforcement, is both a thief taker and a thief. And Godwin, for as much as he represents Gines as the very worst sort of man, basically agrees with his sentiments that "there was no comparison between the liberal and manly profession of a robber . . . and the sordid and mechanical obligation of a blood-hunter" (270). But if Godwin's characterization of Caleb drew from the antispy sentiment demonstrated in the portrayal of Gines, why is Gines so evil and Caleb, at the worst, an irritating upstart? Because it is Godwin's point precisely that Caleb's emergent detective qualities are entirely different from Gines's hounding and self-interested pursuit. Unlike Gines and his spying, representative of a dying civilization,[13] Caleb represents what Godwin advocates in his political writings of the 1780s and 1790s: a modern system of inquiry and observation consistent with English values. Godwin draws a picture of what such a person would look like in another *Morning Chronicle* letter, written the year he was composing *Caleb Williams*. Addressing "such persons as may be appointed to serve upon juries for the trial of seditious and treasonable words," Godwin tells them what he expects:

> One upright and intelligent juryman might put a close to that scene of persecution which is the disgrace of Britain. Let us figure this man to ourselves, contending with the prejudices and passions of his colleagues. Let us figure his mildness and equanimity in the midst of their impatience, and perhaps their scurrility. Let us figure to ourselves that clear, simple, unornamented understanding, which furnishes him with a plain and undeniable answer to all their objections. Let us suppose truth by his instrumentality victorious, not merely over the passions, but over the understanding of united numbers. . . . Integrity never appears more divine in human form, than when it bursts forth from obscurity: than when it appears, unornamented by rank, unassisted by learning, invincible, though alone; than when it disdains circumlocution, tells a plain and artless tale, and shows that all the powers of sophistry and intimidation are impotent, when set in opposition to it. (Marken and Pollin 124)

In its call for and description of the ideal juryman, this passage is both a call for and description of Caleb. Like the juryman who "bursts forth from obscurity" to tell his own "plain and artless tale" against all odds, Caleb tells his with the hope that it does not become, in the final words of the novel, a "half-told and mangled tale" (337). In the final pages of the novel, Falkland concedes defeat in the same words as this passage: "I see that the artless and manly story you have told has carried conviction to every hearer" (335). Godwin develops his earlier description of Cicero's "open and fearless" inquiry here in this portrait of a figure of reason rather than passion and of equanimity in the face of universal hostility, which is clearly a model for Caleb. This model of restraint became the model for the ideal modern detective as he appeared in the propolice treatises of the early-nineteenth century. Critchley describes the code of instructions recruits had then and still have to learn: "He must remember that there is no qualification so indispensable to a police-officer as a perfect command of temper, never suffering himself to be moved in the slightest degree by any language or threats that may be used" (120).

The language describing Caleb's thirst for knowledge echoes this passage's emphasis on "unornamented understanding." Unlike the spying of Gines and Falkland, which is scurrilously motivated by the archaic value of revenge, Caleb's "eagerness for information" (119) springs naturally from him. He writes early in his story that "the spring of action which, perhaps more than any other, characterised the whole train of my life, was curiosity" (6). Like the "curiosity" that Godwin attributed to the public regarding the Hastings affair, Caleb's curiosity is not a vehicle of arbitrary power but a defense against it. The "motive" fueling his duel with "the colossal intelligence of Mr. Falkland" was "the ever-growing repugnance I felt to injustice and arbitrary power" (263). It is crucial for Godwin's reinvention of "spying" as detection, associated not with the crimes of the past century but with the progress of the future one, that Caleb's detection is portrayed as taking place in self-defense, in response to oppression rather than oppression itself. Caleb writes that "the hostility of Mr Falkland excited hostility in me," but like the model juryman, he keeps his head. Like the police will be instructed to do in the face of almost universal hostility, Caleb, "totally abjuring the offensive, [resolves] to stand firmly upon the defensive" (151). Even after Falkland is brought into the courtroom through Caleb's active resolve, the latter maintains "I will not hurt a hair of his head" but significantly adds "unless compelled to it by a principle of defence" (320). This is the logic of modern justice.[14]

Critics are quick to point out that if Godwin's aim was to present Caleb as a reasonable inquirer in the face of Falkland's despotic omniscience, he sometimes missed his mark. Sometimes Caleb's curiosity does indeed look less like Cicero's and more like Gabriel Betteredge's "detective fever" in *The Moonstone*. Passages such as the one in which Caleb, on the verge of discovering Falkland's secret, exclaims "I felt as if my animal system had undergone a total revolution. My blood boiled within me" (135) support critical arguments to the effect that the detective narrative is at heart a psychological not a political exploration. Godwin's text does not always seem entirely sure, given "things as they are," where Caleb's spirit of inquiry will lead him, giving us reason to think that the uncertainty demonstrated by the novel's two endings, the original and the published, derails whatever sure-footed social critique Godwin may have intended. This uncertainty, however, is not a self-limiting paradox in Godwin's reform politics, hopelessly torn between (1) wanting to make a consistent critique of "things" by having Caleb crushed by an eternally unjust system (original ending), or (2) wanting justice to stage a victory by having Falkland confess, thus vindicating Caleb's social criticism even as it brings out the least attractive aspects of Caleb's personality (published ending). The need for two endings makes sense if Godwin's text, as I argue, is borne on the cusp of an emergent cultural logic, a logic defined by the attempt to reconcile the intrusions required by detective work with the freedom held dear by the English people. Just as Caleb's new detective work both separates him from and links him to the reviled spying of Gines, a logic associated with the "new" necessarily draws from a critique of the old. Some critics have recognized Caleb as a "cusp" figure. Marilyn Butler points out that part of the problem in "reading" Caleb is that there is not at this time "a vocabulary to justify what he does" (248). Gary Handwerk underscores the emergent nature of Godwin's logic in explaining why Falkland is so much more readable than his curious servant: "*Caleb Williams* never provides the same sort of explanatory context for Caleb as it does for Falkland. . . . Caleb remains a remarkably isolated individual, literally an orphan, inhabiting a world free of conscious ideological resonances" (952). The novel's at times uncomfortable balance between a fully drawn attack on things as they are and a sketchy program for things as they can be are not doubts but growing pains. If Godwin seemed less sure-footed in his writings in the 1790s than in the 1780s, it may just be that he got ahead of himself. After all, Caleb embodies the ideals of the Victorian detective, "unornamented understanding" and dogged, rational inquiry, almost forty years before England would officially create one.

The History of British India AND DETECTION

If Godwin, in writing *Caleb Williams,* was picking up where he left off in his Empire writings, James Mill's Empire writings pick up where *Caleb Williams* leaves off, thus producing what Godwin's arguably less prescriptive text could not: suggestions for the construction of the English detective. While it is hard to imagine Mill, driven by the demands of his equally voluminous writing project and family, feverishly turning the pages of *Caleb Williams* to see if the plucky servant (for whom he would certainly root) managed to bring down his tyrannical master, Mill's text resonates with the logic and language of Godwin's. In his *History*, Mill tries to reverse the "dangerous tendency of . . . representing districts, or things, to be in a more favourable state than they really are": "It is necessary to have studied particularly the documents of our Indian history . . . to have any conception to what an extent the British people have been deluded, and continue to be deluded, with flattering accounts of what is described as 'their empire in India'" (5:405–6). Mill goes on to argue, like Godwin, that the problem with India is that there has been no "enlightened enquirer" to bring simple understanding and inspection to the subcontinent. In other words, the problem with British India is that it has no Caleb Williams. The solution offered by *The History of British India* is to create one in the form of the new East India Company servant, especially the policeman armed with local knowledge of Indian culture and general knowledge of English law.

As with Godwin, so much of Mill's criticism of imperial policy is at heart a critique of domestic policy that any argument against colonial mismanagement is bound to become a recipe for better domestic governance. Like Godwin, Mill consequently weaves a constructive program for the future from savage attacks on the present. Mill suggests in his preface that the true patriot must be cruel to be kind. "Some considerable reputations have been acquired," he writes, "by praising every thing in one's own country. . . . And that it is a proof of his not being a friend to it, if he ever puts it in the wrong. This is a motive which I utterly disclaim" (1:xxxiii–xxxiv). Like the misunderstood Caleb's pursuit of the popular Falkland, Mill's motive in making accusations of criminality against popular institutions in the face of widespread hostility is "to be a friend to one's country" (1:xxxiv).

Mill is not considered a friend to any country. The standard view of Mill is that he takes the boldly arrogant position that India can be known and ruled from afar. Horace Hayman Wilson, an Oxford Orientalist and the 1840 editor of *The History*, writes in his preface that "Mr. Mill does not seem to have been aware" that "personal knowledge of a country, and especially of India" is necessary for writing an accurate history (1:ix). Leslie Stephen, in his account of the English Utilitarians, writes of Mill's "prejudices" that they were "characteristic of the Utilitarian attitude to assume that a sufficient knowledge of fact can always be obtained from bluebooks and statistics. Some facts require imagination and sympathy to be appreciated, and there Mill was deficient" (2:23–24). In being so unfamiliar with the actual country, according to Wilson, Mill is a flawed historian and social critic. Only someone with "local knowledge. . . . will know what to credit, what to mistrust, what to disbelieve. He will be qualified to select the pure metal from the dross, to separate the false from the true. An incompetency to perform this most essential part of the duties of a careful and critical historian is constantly apparent in the citations which Mr. Mill has made" (1:viii–ix).

While Mill is not without sometimes astonishing prejudices, the point that he is making in *The History of British India,* both as a reformer and as an historian, challenges this standard reading. The central tenet of Mill's argument about British India is the necessity for such local knowledge in the development of good government. In a note referring to a passage about the "mode of conducting" the Company's business, he writes:

> Where the agent, however, is intelligent, and acquainted with the language and the manners of the people, he does simplify and improve the business to a certain degree; and were it performed by men who had an interest to establish themselves in the country, and who would make it a business, it would gradually acquire that rational form which the interest of a rational people would recommend. (3:11)

Mill himself implies a connection between the work of the "intelligent agent" and his work as an historian.

> In the course of reading and investigation, necessary for acquiring that measure of knowledge which I was anxious to possess, respecting my country, its people, its government, its interests, its policy, and its laws, I was met, and in some degree surprised, by extraordinary difficulties, when I arrived at that part of my inquiries which related to India. . . . The knowledge, requisite for attaining an adequate conception of that great scene of British action, was collected no where. It was scattered in a great variety of repositories. (1:xv)

Turning the "dispersed and confused materials of a knowledge of India" into a "rational form" is Mill's attempt, in Caleb's words, to turn a "half-told and mangled tale" (337) into a plain and artless one.

Mill's text, like Godwin's, is a criticism of criminal law that frequently references contemporary accounts of criminal justice reform. Mill, too, cites Howard on the savagery of English prisons (3:117). Though Mill's text is a history and therefore organizes itself chronologically while chronicling wars, government, and Company policy and important personnel, his intense and energetic focus on crime and the police, as opposed to these other aspects of British India, makes his history sometimes read like a colonial edition of the *Newgate Calendar*. Mill writes exhaustively of both Indian and English crimes; he covers the iniquities of the "dacoits," Indian criminal gangs, with the same kind of salacious detail that spices up his account of the Hastings trial, which focuses on English crimes from mismanagement to murder.

The Hastings administration is the focus of Mill's criticism of justice in British India. Two hundred pages are devoted to the trial, with numerous additional references and asides elsewhere in the text. Mill's account of the trial's crime-within-a-crime, the execution of Nuncomar, sounds like a *Caleb Williams* plot summary: servant accuses master thereby becoming the accused.[15] Nuncomar accused Hastings in 1775 of accepting a large bribe from one of the Begums of Oudh, at which point the Brahmin was arrested for an alleged forgery. The Supreme Court in Calcutta, presided over by Hastings's school friend, Sir Elijah Impey, tried and executed Nuncomar, thus conveniently removing Hastings's accuser. Hastings is represented here as a Falkland, who will do anything in his power to block inquiry into his actions. Mill's portrayal of "the eagerness of the Governor-General to stifle, and his exertions to obstruct inquiry, on all occasions where his conduct came under complaint" echoes Godwin's description of Falkland's fatal flaw (3:443). As Falkland is reluctantly brought before Mr. Forester, Falkland's half brother and Caleb's fair-weather friend, so Hastings resents inquiry. Mill quotes Hastings's declaration that "I will not suffer Nuncomar to appear before the Board as my accuser. I know what belongs to the dignity and character of the first member of this administration. I will not sit at this Board in the character of criminal" (3:447). Hastings stands accused of the same crime as Falkland, who preempted Caleb's charges of criminality against him by accusing Caleb first of theft. Falkland, implicitly describing his own strategy as he explicitly charges Caleb, exclaims that "surely it is no sufficient refutation of a criminal charge, that the criminal repels what is alleged against him" (177). Hastings's attempts at "stifling inquiry," according to Mill, use a similar strategy: "What [Hastings] alleged was, the dignity of the accused, and the baseness of the accuser" (3:447). While Nuncomar and Caleb meet very different fates (if only in the published ending), the single crime of Hastings/Falkland is the obstruction of the spirit of inquiry through a strategy of preemptive criminalization. The endeavor of defenders of the current system, Mill explains, to "establish in the minds of their countrymen . . . a belief, that it is criminal ever to express blame of them or their system. . . . Has hardly been less diligent than it has been successful" (5:216).

Mill turns from his reading of the Hastings trial to a lengthy discussion of the police system in India, which, in its considerations of both effective and ineffective police work, echoes Godwin's distinction between the work of Gines and Caleb and anticipates crucial arguments for propolice reformers. As in the rogue Regency state of which it is a product, Mill explains, the current state of policing in India is bad. Mill draws practically all of his evidence from the grim "Fifth Report of the Committee on Indian Affairs" (1810), and the criticisms echo contemporaneous assaults on the state of domestic policing in which the police are themselves criminals. "The fabrication of evidence," Mill writes, has become "a prevailing practice with the agents of police" (5:402). Mill suggests that "when such are the deeds of the very men by whom the crimes of others are to be suppressed" there can be no security in British India (5:402). Guilty of the same crime as Hastings and Falkland, police agents, instead of "protectors, themselves became the plunderers and murderers of the people" (5:413). Underscoring his main point about English criminal law—its "deceptive propensity"—Mill argues, here quoting the Fifth Report, that the major obstacle to police reform in India stems from "the very imperfect information which government . . . possessed, respecting the actual state of the police" (5:405). Curiosity, and its by-product, information, are here, too, the necessary instruments for reform.

Mill's solution, comparable to Godwin's, is to replace an old and ignorant system, associated with un-English values of treachery and obfuscation, with a new one characterized by "unornamented" understanding and justice. Mill writes that the Indian police suffer from "a general neglect of duty, in petty rogueries, in a want of respectability, in being destitute of that energy and activity, and that delicate sensibility to character, which ought to characterize a police officer" (5:400). Though Mill is critical of Pitt's 1784 India Bill, he gives credit to the "authors of the bill" for their efforts "to force out the real state of the facts, and to defeat the efforts of concealment or deception. . . . Information tending to the detection of falsehood was called for by the greatest rewards" (4:406). Mill, recognizing as Godwin did that his foreign policy recommendations had domestic implications, adds "so important an instrument of good government as this, ought not, assuredly, to be confined to India" (4:406). Indeed, Mill's criticisms of the police in India are those being made by reformers in a domestic context, as I will argue in the final section of this chapter.

While the nature of Caleb's knowledge has a certain precision—his perfect pitch for dialect and disguise anticipate the celebrated skills of later detectives—Godwin is vague about the institutional position of the detective figure. More often, Godwin refers to principles of "general inspection" or discusses "the duties of individuals . . . to be indefatigable in detecting [society's] imperfections" (1985 545, 661). In the context of actual policy recommendations for improving imperial governance, Mill hones this "general inspection" to an argument for local knowledge, and thus an argument for administrative specialization.[16] In arguing for a local knowledge that becomes specialist in character, Mill adds a key component to the emerging detective narrative Godwin developed. The following passage about the need for local knowledge, particularly regarding the administration of justice, reflects scores of such passages in *The History*:

> Even in the native country of the Judge, experience gained from long practice in the modes of thinking, acting, and speaking, of the principal class of depredators, is found to give him important advantages in extracting the evidence of guilt. The extraordinary disadvantages, under which Englishmen, totally unacquainted with the manners of the Indians, lie, when they begin to seek their way through the labyrinth of Indian testimony, can be easily conceived. (5:436)

Here Mill advocates a system whereby Englishmen would become proto-Kimball O'Haras, "thoroughly conversant with the manners and character of the natives: many of them born and bred among them" (5:437). Mill's proposals to rectify this problem with local and specialized inquiry, Stokes explains, "had all those qualities of energy, speed, efficiency, and decisiveness, dear to the reformer's heart" (79–80). This argument for better administration through local knowledge is one that will be made by such reformers about the New Police in London.

The figure of the English agent "thoroughly conversant with the . . . character of the natives" is clearly the solution to a criminal law at home and abroad, which currently smites "the administration of the justice with impotence." However, the "vices of the law" are only one part of the problem. The second cause are those problems "which derive themselves from the vices of the people" of India (5:431). And it is here where Mill begins to make clear the national investments in the figure of the detective in a way that Godwin only implied. The type of cultural superiority evinced in this matter-of-fact statement is not surprising, following, as it does, Mill's infamous attack on Hindu civilization. However, such an arraignment of the native population is surprising for a text that, for the most part, works harder at indicting English civilization. Wilson, the editor, notes that "one of our author's peculiarities" is that "his horror of English is even more strong than of Hindu law" (2:362).

Mill's attack on native culture is paradoxical: While it resonates with similar dismissals of the achievements of Indian culture (Macaulay's "Minute on
Indian Education"[17] being the most famous and formative example), the
whole purpose of *The History* is to argue not for a wholesale rejection but
rather a greater and more detailed knowledge of India, possessed by newly
respectable agents. Such interpretative difficulty recalls the quandary traditional criticism confronted in trying to decide why and how the two endings
to *Caleb Williams* destabilized the author's argument. Reading Mill's *History*
as part of an emerging detective genre sheds some light on this paradox. In
view of the tensions between moderation and force troubling nineteenth-century arguments for the police, Mill's attack on the Hindus can be seen as uni-
fying rather than derailing his argument, as the emerging detective narrative
spells out the new imperial logic. If India's rogue citizenry can be ordered by
a new kind of English investigation, then this new detective figure can claim
precisely those qualities the English public would not grant the work of
detection: that it was both necessary and good.

Mill's call for local knowledge on the part of Englishmen in India represents
itself as a necessary response to a grave social problem. Much like Hastings and
Falkland in this respect, Mill uses his understanding of the essential criminality of the subject population to defend his call for greater authority.[18] While
the dacoits are an object of particular attention, the general population is
almost as dangerous. "Dissimulation and falsehood, the universal concomi-
tants of oppression" are carried by the Hindus to "a height almost unexampled
among the other races of men" (1:324). Just as Caleb converts spying into
detection through self-defense, Mill makes English detective work necessary to
social self-defense in the face of the essential deceptiveness of Indian culture.
Mill argues that a better police system is more important in India, where the
native character does not provide a margin for error:

> A system of law, marked by so many infirmities, may, in a country like
> England, where crimes are easily suppressed, and where the sentiments and
> manners of the people accomplish more than the law, afford an appearance
> of efficacy, and get the credit of much of that order which it does not pro-
> duce; but in a country like India, where crimes are difficult to repress, and
> where the law receives little aid from the sentiments and manners of the peo-
> ple, a far more perfect system is required. (5:398)

The necessity of a centralized police force to right social wrongs was a position strenuously resisted by the English public at the time Mill was writing.
The context of Empire provided Mill with a vehicle for mounting an argu-

ment that he could not mount within the context of domestic social reform. Debates about police reform in India contained in the Fifth Report repeatedly underscored that the "powers" granted overseas would not be tolerated at home. These are powers "which never have been confided to any subordinate peace-officers in England: and which, indeed, would not be tolerated for a moment in that country" (5:403). Given that Mill's focus on the essential criminality of India grew out of a condemnation of English law, however, it should come as no surprise that the argument for the necessity of the police in India eventually found its way back home. Mill's representation of the acquisition of knowledge as social self-defense in the context of an imperial world was in place by the time propolice reformers began to argue for the police in the increasingly "imperial" metropolis of London.

GODWIN, MILL, AND THE NEW POLICE

The writings of John Wade, one of the most widely read police advocates of the early-nineteenth century, illustrate how the divergent political philosophies of Godwin and Mill found a home in formative arguments for a New Police. Wade, a former journeyman wool sorter turned journalist and political writer, edited the *Gorgon* under the direction of Francis Place (a good friend of both Godwin and Mill) and wrote numerous books on issues central to radical legal reform, such as *The Extraordinary Black Book* (1820–1823), *The Cabinet Lawyer* (1826), *A Treatise on the Police and Crimes of the Metropolis* (1829), and *History of the Middle and Working Classes* (1835).[1'] The following discussion of the emerging argument for a police system in England focuses on Wade's *Treatise,* and another influential argument for the police, George B. Mainwaring's *Observations on the Present State of the Police of the Metropolis* (1821). Coming in the 1820s, Wade's and Mainwaring's texts utilize an argument that, thanks to Godwin and Mill, was already in place. These reform writings show how Godwin's and Mill's new stories of English criminal justice shaped the reimagination of the English police.

The police in the early nineteenth century had an identity crisis in which, in the words of Caleb, "innocence and guilt [were] too much confounded" (122). Official considerations of England's confounded policing echo the observations of Godwin and Mill. Mainwaring argues:

> The most superficial observer of the external and visible appearances of this town, must soon be convinced, that there is a large mass of unproductive population living upon it. . . . differing little from the barbarous hordes

which traverse an uncivilized land. . . . This, too, in the midst of a wealthy,
highly civilized and refined city, the capital of a country blessed with the best
Constitution on earth; a Constitution, whose laws have been said to provide
a remedy for every wrong. (4–5)

And yet an unregulated system of quasi-criminal thief takers, as the unoffi-
cial police were seen to be, seemed shabby defenders of the "best
Constitution on earth." In the words of the 1822 Select Committee on the
Police of the Metropolis, a police force is "difficult to reconcile . . . with that
perfect freedom of action and exemption from interference, which are the
great privileges and blessings of society in this country" (qtd. in Radzinowicz
1:588). Mainwaring concurs that "the character" of the police was "not
favourable to its investment with that degree of authority without which it
cannot now be beneficial to the public" (11). Sir Robert Peel, who knew the
efficacy of an organized police force first hand from his tenure in Ireland,
summed up the dilemma in an 1828 letter to Henry Hobhouse: "What must
I do with the Police? I fear throughout the whole country it is most defective.
. . . It has always appeared to me that the country has entirely out-grown its
police institutions" (qtd. in Radzinowicz 1:588).

While they vigorously disagreed about particulars, all these reformers, rad-
ical and Tory alike, agreed that the country was changing in ways that cast
doubt on England's legitimacy as an imperial authority. That England needed a police force was not a new idea. Many of the actual recommendations
Peel put into law had been around since the 1750s, in the writings of the
Fielding brothers, and particularly since the 1790s, in the work of magistrate
Patrick Colquhoun. So why did these arguments finally take hold in 1829?
After the writings of Godwin and Mill, recommendations about the police
could speak in the reassuring rather than revolutionary language of an existing argument. Godwin's and Mill's accounts of "things as they are" helped to
establish the parameters of the winning argument that local knowledge could
be embodied in a figure responsible to and therefore reconcilable with the
interest of an expanding nation.

The propolice narratives clearly use Godwin's and Mill's strategies of con-
trasting an effective new system with ineffectual old ones. Wade writes of the
new police system that "it would speedily be found as much superior to the
old parochial machinery, as the steam and iron pipes of the New River
Company are to the wooden troughs and creaking wheels of the late London
Bridge water-works" (96). Indeed, an anonymous barrister, writing a few
years before Wade, uses the same symbols of modern progress to suggest that,
regarding the police, England is woefully behind the times: "We are almost

as far behind hand in the knowledge of police, considered as science, as though we had for the first time turned our attention to the properties of steam, when the engine had been at work for years in every other part of Europe" (qtd. in Radzinowicz 3:413).

Propolice reformers take up the argument sketched out by Godwin and Mill that it was increasingly the "duty of the state to know."[20] According to Wade, police "ought to be intimately acquainted with the localities of their jurisdiction, and the prevailing character of the population, their occupations, amusements, and habits" (9). In addition, Wade continues, "a general knowledge of all the arts of fraud, imposture, and depredation" is "a qualification which can hardly be derived from education, and can only result from observation, or perhaps natural gift. . . . The power of discriminating criminal character" (10). Mainwaring, who criticized the archaic "nightly watch" because it kept the police in bed all day and thereby prevented them from acquiring a knowledge of "the bad characters upon the town . . . a knowledge indispensable to an effective officer" (52), suggests that knowledge needs to be locally gathered and then organized. Information needs to be organized, according to influential reformer Edwin Chadwick, to keep "information gained in one district" from being "lost to all others" (qtd. in Radzinowicz 2:199). Such arguments were persuasive; according to Michael Ignatieff, "by the early 1820s, the society had concluded that the legitimacy of state institutions could only be safeguarded by centralization of control and administration by professionals" (168).

However, as we have already seen, the modern solution of locally acquired, centrally organized knowledge walks a fine line between qualities variously seen as alternately safeguarding and threatening the English character.[21] "Reform could have been a disastrous failure," Critchley explains, "had not the architects of the 'New Police' been scrupulously careful to set up an institution exactly matched to the British temperament" (119). Mainwaring argues that police emanate from rather than antagonize the principles of the Constitution:

> Whilst the people preserve their Constitution, they need not fear a police. . . . the genius, the habits of the people, the succession to authorities, and the interest in the administration of the laws amongst the middling classes of society, seem almost designed to furnish a description of persons suited to our police establishment. (55–64)

These are the qualities Godwin called for in his juryman and drew upon in his portrayal of Caleb. Mainwaring's description of the "primary requisite

. . . of a constable's duty," "a judicious mind, a peaceable temper, a reserved demeanour, with the necessary resolution in extremity" (64), echoes Caleb's longsuffering endurance of persecution and the logic behind his two public accusations of Falkland.

One of the characteristics found in both Godwin's and Mill's early articulation of the logic of the police is that the English spirit of inquiry is a defensive rather than an offensive methodology. The paradoxical characterization of state intervention as primarily defensive, symbolizing protection from threat rather than the threat itself, shaped the Victorian reimagination of modern justice.[22] Godwin and Mill could not make their arguments about the nation's defense outside the context of Empire, whether it was in the need for inquiry to defend against assaults on English principles from (1) an outdated criminal justice system, (2) English criminals such as Hastings, or (3) Indian ones such as Mill's criminal Hindus. The context of Empire is as crucial for arguments about domestic policing. We have already seen Mainwaring's use of the barbarous/civilized distinction to represent the dangers of an unpoliced London. Wade, too, squarely places the challenges of law enforcement in the context of Empire. He explains that "a vigilance and suspicion which would be wholly superfluous in a provincial town are indispensable to the safety and regulation of a vast metropolis" because in "England, more than in any European community, is a numerous class enjoying, or, rather, labouring under, a plethora of wealth, the produce of vast colonial possessions" (7,14). Vigilance is necessary, not only because of colonial wealth but because of the increased presence of colonial subjects. The first cause of the rise of mendacity is, according to Wade, "the influx of strangers from every part of the United Kingdom, from the Colonies and foreign parts" (137). But it is the imperial dimension of the British character—the Crusoe gene—as well that leads to the rise of crime: "The avidity of mercantile adventure" to which Englishmen are characteristically prone, Wade explains, contributes to "the magnitude and complexion of our criminal calendar" (219,100).

Like Godwin and Mill, Wade points out in his *Treatise* that certain threats to national security stem from the global dimensions of English civilization. Like Godwin and Mill, Wade's solution for this problem is the necessary work of the police: an English spirit of inquiry. Wade contributes to the story of the detective told by Godwin and Mill by employing both Godwin's model of a gradual extension of liberty with a "rational enquirer" at the center and Mill's model of good government with a judicial specialist at the center. In the final words of his *Treatise*, Wade continues the balancing act of the detective narrative that will be picked up by future writers, such as Dickens, in the continuing work of reimagining the police as necessary defense in an imperial world. Wade comments on Peel's recently passed Metropolitan Police Act of 1829:

> Since concluding our work a Police-Bill has been introduced, in which we recognize the commencement of a better system of protective justice, and an attempt to introduce that energy and consolidation of power which we have shown to be essential to public security. Though the new measure of the Right Hon. Secretary of State is of limited extent, and intended to operate gradually, we apprehend the powers it confers, if fully and judiciously executed, will accomplish important improvements in the Metropolitan Police. (369)

We have seen the work these reformers had to do to be able to write such a paragraph. They had to be able to associate the police with a progressive protective center rather than an assault on Englishness if they were going to propose a police that could be read as a metropolitan invention that will "operate gradually" and naturally outward from the center. As my account of Godwin and Mill suggests, however, this new concept of English criminal justice is one that worked its way back to the metropolitan center from the colonial periphery. Godwin's novel is one of the first texts to imagine how an investigation of imperial authority, whether that of Hastings, Alexander, or Falkland, might restore credibility to English justice. Moreover, to take a good look at England, Godwin suggests, requires us to look outside its borders. Subsequent arguments like Mill's and the later work of reformers thus ensure that Godwin's tale does not suffer the fate of Caleb's in the original ending of the novel but rather presents us with an understanding of the Englishness of detective work that is still with us today. In the original ending, Caleb's tale is heard only by the walls of his prison cell. But Godwin's revised ending gives Caleb the floor at the center of an English courtroom, insuring that the message of *Caleb Williams* would be heard loud and clear by even the passionate skeptics at the center of the emerging empire.

≒2≒

THUGGEE AND THE "DISCOVERY"
OF THE ENGLISH DETECTIVE

T
he first fully-imagined English detective is not found in *Bleak House* or on Baker Street, but rather in India. William Sleeman, the first superintendent of the Thug Police, an intelligence operation developed in the 1820s and 1830s, is this New Man. How could the Thug Police—in the space of a single decade—become the type of "enlightened inquirers" called for by Godwin, Mill, and the propolice reformers influenced by them? While the phenomenon of Thuggee seemed to provide a new story about a mysterious India, it in fact enabled a new story to be told about the emergent yet already embattled English police.

The story of Sleeman and his small band of men in the Thuggee and Dacoity Department is told in the many narratives about the crime of Thuggee and its suppression, widely read at the dawn of Victoria's reign: works by Sleeman himself, Edward Thornton's *Illustrations of the History and Practices of the Thugs* (1837), Caleb Wright's *Lectures on India* (1849), Henry H. Spry's *Modern India* (1837), Fanny Parks's *The Wanderings of a Pilgrim in Search of the Picturesque* (1850), Charles Hervey's *Some Records of Crime* (1892), articles in the *Edinburgh Review* and *Blackwood's Magazine,* and most famously Captain Philip Meadows Taylor's best selling novel, *Confessions of a Thug* (1839), a particular favorite of the young Queen.[1] These narratives detail in a suggestively uniform manner the habits, customs, superstitions, and peculiar vocabulary of the Thugs, centuries-old Indian gangs whose "special service" to the goddess Kali, "one of the dark divinities of the Hindoo creed" (Wright 141), allegedly led them to roam the country strangling and robbing Indian travelers. The narratives' wealth of detail, culled from Thug confessions, was organized into maps of Thug travel patterns, Thug family trees, an extensive glossary of the Thug vocabulary, "Ramasi," and studies of Thug phrenology.[2] The phenomenon of Thuggee represents a crucial moment in the evolution of intelligence-based police work and in the English understanding and representation of their role in India.

Treatments of detective fiction, invested in the detective novel as a home-grown genre and in Englishness as a stable identity, have traditionally ignored the important work done in police history by Mike Brogden and others to write in the "critical *imperial* context of police origins." An "insular histori-ography" results in such oversights as the importance of Thuggee in the devel-opment of the English police and is complemented by its seeming opposite: totalizing readings of the extension of British authority in the colonies. Recent readings of Thuggee, in the context not of detective fiction but of imperial writing as a whole, see in the Thuggee narratives evidence of an unproblematic extension of imperial panopticism and as a result the neat pro-duction of English cops and Indian robbers, a compartmentalization that seems perfectly to accord with our contemporary understanding of crime and punishment in British India, informed as it is by the stark midcentury bru-tality of the Mutiny and its suppression.

However, the narratives of the detection and suppression of Thuggee chal-lenge both these accounts of English authority (entirely local and effortlessly global) and afford a reexamination of the emergence of the detective, the detective narrative, and the production of colonial policy in an age less of ret-ribution than reform. Unlike the gradual diffusion of English values from the metropolis outward represented in the Whiggish histories of the police and the detective genre, the colonial context of the rapid detection of Thuggee and, crucially, the Thuggee narratives' organization of this detective work into popular, readable accounts, enabled the bad turn-of-the-century cop to become good, to become English, and therefore to come home to a more receptive public. Even as the Thuggee narratives invalidate a strictly home-grown police history, they equally complicate readings of an always already confident imperial power. In other words, efforts against Thuggee might seem to provide a platform for an unprecedented and public display of the new detective at work against rampant Indian criminality. However, far from the sure-footed panopticism argued in both older and recent readings of Thug policing, the Thug Police gingerly enter a stage set not by British jin-goism but by the contested liberalism evident in contemporary police debates, in which the fear of excessive police authority taints the case then being made for them as emanations of the true liberal spirit of the English constitution.[3]

Some of these critics are not ultimately incorrect. Representations of Thuggee do participate in shaping the new stories of English justice and

Indian criminality and leave the old story of English judicial criminality in its
wake. Accepting the Thug Police as English, however, also requires accepting
a new story of English culture, one that registers the imbrication rather than
the clear distinction between two identities, liberal and authoritarian, and
two worlds, Metropolitan England and the colonial periphery. For if in the
Thuggee narratives the detective emerges as a necessary figure who through
his "local knowledge" interprets the data and solves the mysteries of the
Empire for an English reading public, he is necessarily an imperial rather than
an insularly English invention.

   This chapter will examine what stories the Thuggee narratives tell about
India and the English police. I am especially interested in how the detective
narrative emerges as a new form to organize these often contesting cultural
stories. The first section shows how representations of Thuggee criminalize
Indian culture and establish a crucial identification between the English reading public and the work of the police. The second section documents the
challenge of the Thug Police in making this new story of police authority
credible. The third section explains how both the character of the detective
and the genre of detective fiction attempt to confront the question of credibility haunting applications of state power and, in addressing this problem,
cast the narrative mission for the Victorian detective novel.

THE STORY OF THE THUGS

Accounts of Thuggee routinely conflate Thuggee and India. Such a slippage
is evident in the comments of traveler and writer Fanny Parks, a friend and
visitor of William Sleeman at Jubbolpore, the location of the largest Thug
prison. Parks writes that Thuggee is

> no sooner suppressed than a new system of secret assassination and robbery
> is discovered, proving the truth of Colonel [William] Sleeman's remark that
> "India is a strange land; and live in it as long as we may, and mix with its peo-
> ple as much as we please, we shall to the last be constantly liable to stumble
> upon new moral phenomena to excite our special wonder". (James Sleeman
> 194)

Here, in the space of one sentence, the story of mysterious criminal practices
has become the story of the "strange land" of India. Caleb Wright continually makes this equation between Thuggee and Indian culture as a whole by
emphasizing how the "occupation" of "the cold-blooded miscreants who, in

India, make a trade of assassination" is "sanctioned by the national religion" (141). The Thuggee texts recount multiple stories of Indians who are both Thugs *and* successful members of the mainstream community, such as the infamous master Thug who was by day a respectable and quite accomplished linen draper. The "ramifications" of Thuggee, Thornton cries, "are so widely-extended, and reach so far into the very heart of Indian society" that it is "almost inconceivable." But in case his readers were actually to find it inconceivable, Thornton continues, "It would strike us as extraordinary, if tradesmen in Cheapside or Bond Street united with their respective occupations that of murder: yet this state of things exists in India" (468).

According to these texts, Thuggee is able to be so "widely-extended" throughout Indian culture because of its relation to the dominant religion, Hinduism.[4] This association with religion gives Thuggee its fearful eternal character as well. The central precept of this "religion of murder," as it is often called, is that once a Thug, always a Thug. Ameer Ali, the hero of Taylor's novel *Confessions of a Thug*, describes the "goor," the coarse sugar used in Thug rituals, as symbolizing a point of no return. "I have eaten the Goor," he says, "and cannot change" (14). Thornton quotes a Thug, who confesses to Sleeman that while "we all feel pity sometimes . . . the goor of the Tuponee changes our nature; it would change the nature of a horse. Let any man once taste of that goor and he will be a Thug, though he . . . [has] all the wealth in the world" (66).

Though everywhere and eternal, Thuggee is by definition deceptive and thus maddeningly hidden from imperial eyes. Even the Thug method for killing has developed with an aim toward greater concealment, moving from a lasso to a sash, which can be better concealed on the body. These accounts dwell on the great pains taken by Thugs to avoid discovery. Thugs kill all members of the traveling party to insure that no one survives who could testify against them. In a detail sure to inflame the English reading public, the dogs of the victims are also killed. To prevent the bodies from swelling and being discovered in their shallow graves, the already strangled corpses are stabbed in the stomach and the armpits.[5] Once again, the narratives represent this deception as indicative of Indian rather than exclusively Thug culture. Trevelyan looks to a Hindu proverb, "there is darkness under the lamp," for an explanation as to how "a whole family with their servants could be murdered . . . without any discovery taking place" (360). Thuggee, a "habitual system of deception" that justifies itself as a religious practice, is represented as an accepted part of secular culture as well. Exasperated colonial administrators complain that without the widespread protection offered by paid-off princes and native officials Thuggee could not exist. "This tolerance of professional thieves and

murderers," Thornton suggests, "is a remarkable feature in the phenomena of
Indian society" (433). And a feature, Parks suggests, which will only become
more widespread in the absence of English authority: "In the territories of the
native chiefs of Bundelcund, and those of Scindia and Holcar, a Thug feels just
as independent and free as an Englishman in a tavern, and they will probably
begin to feel themselves just as much so in those of Nagpore, now that
European superintendency has been withdrawn" (1:157).[6]

It becomes clear throughout these narratives that in discovering these
widely extended truths about the fundamental and furtive lawlessness of
Indian culture, certain aspects of English culture, more essential even than a
fondness for taverns, are simultaneously revealed. The English perceive themselves as essentially law abiding. Trevelyan explains, "If any practice at all
approaching in atrocity to that of Thuggee were to be discovered in England,
it would be immediately put down by an united effort of the whole people"
(393). One of the contemporary arguments against an organized police force
in England was that an official force was unnecessary because there was a little natural policeman in all Englishmen. But in the colonial context of widespread indigenous crime, it easily becomes an argument for the necessary
association of policing with Englishness, an association Parks makes above.[7]

Given this association, it follows that one of the most consistent features of
these Thuggee narratives is a progress report on the British efforts against
Thuggee, illustrated here in the title of Thornton's *Illustrations of the History
and Practices of the Thugs: And Notices of Some of the Proceedings of the
Government of India, for the Suppression of the Crime of Thuggee*. Captain Taylor
explains in the introduction to *Confessions of a Thug* that "the Confessions I
have recorded are not published to gratify a morbid taste in any one for tales
of horror and of crime; they were written. . . . to awaken public vigilance in
the suppression of Thuggee" (xxiii). As the frequent final chapter of these
Thuggee narratives, police work ultimately becomes a model for organizing the
often bewildering imperial experience for English readers and creates a link
between detective work and the readers' work based on a shared curiosity.
Indeed, it seems the reader is almost deputized in the writer's call for participation. Practically all the Thuggee narratives open with a call for "public vigilance in the suppression of Thuggee" (Philip Taylor xxiii).[8] Frederick Holme,
writing in *Blackwood's* about Thuggee, echoes Godwin's argument concerning
the importance of English curiosity about Indian affairs:

> the astounding disclosures relative to the system of secret murder in India,
> called *Thuggee*, which have been brought to light during the last ten years,
> have so far penetrated the veil of apathy through which every detail regard-

ing our Indian empire is too generally contemplated in this country, as to excite a considerable degree of curiosity in the listless minds of *general readers*. (229)

The emphasis on curiosity as an essentially English characteristic is central to reversing the stigma attached to detective work. Most histories of the police in the nineteenth century argue that intelligence does not emerge as a policing technique, due to an English distaste for spying, until the creation of the Criminal Investigation Department (CID) at the end of the 1880s.[9] Public hatred of spying did shape the representation of the police. But rather than delay the use of intelligence in policing, such public antipathy simply mandated that intelligence be represented as a visible extension of individual curiosity, rather than a hidden tool of the state. William Sleeman's curiosity is shown to be exhaustive, as he explains in the preface to *Ramaseeana* that

> I have entered in this Vocabulary every thing to which Thugs in any part of India have thought it necessary to assign a peculiar term. . . . I am satisfied that there is no term, no rite, no ceremony, no opinion, no omen or usage that they have intentionally concealed from me. (75)

Sleeman used his research to construct family trees for the Thugs, and according to his biographer and grandson, "with these genealogical trees to work upon, [operated] the machinery for its suppression. . . . [and the] equally arduous task of obtaining the necessary evidence, since . . . even the most notorious Thug had to have a fair trial" (James Sleeman 194). This description not only demonstrates the innovation and ardor of Sleeman's curiosity but also his ability to reconcile this new police work with the traditional demands of British fair play. Both colonial administrators and English readers can relate to Sleeman's work.

The Thuggee narratives' emphasis on curiosity introduces the Thug Police's method—detection as organized curiosity—as one already acceptable by English readers because it is what the English readers are in fact doing in reading about the Thugs. This connection between police and readers underscores how important widespread public interest in the police was in the replacement of the old story of secretive rogue justice with the new one of modern inquiry.[10] As the curious reader faces the mysteries faced by the curious Thug Police, these narratives introduce readers not only to the detective's motivation but involve them in his method by giving them a massive amount of "evidence" in the form of miscellaneous "facts" about the Thugs, and then leading them to the whole system each piece of evidence partially suggests.[11]

The colonial context of Thuggee, a systematic and hidden crime, enables the activity formerly feared as spying to become modern detection, the embodiment of English curiosity and common sense. The activity formerly feared as a threat to local autonomy, centralization of police, here, too, becomes a uniquely English skill. Sleeman's "general principle" was "to keep under every officer's hand the latest and most completely detailed information," which the Government would print and distribute and the prolific Sleeman would publish for public consumption several times in subsequent years (Tuker 61). Trevelyan describes the aptitude of England, the "supreme power" in India, for "collect[ing] for one common effort the resources of the whole of India, and direct[ing] that effort by European intelligence, energy and perseverance" (368). This is the same argument being made at home for an increasingly centralized police system, indeed one increasingly based on the Thug Police's model of police "intelligence." In fact John Ward makes this argument just one year later than Trevelyan did in the same journal, the *Edinburgh Review.* In his progress report on the "Police of the Metropolis," Ward argues that no police system "can be perfect until a regular chain of communication, under one central authority, is kept up throughout the whole kingdom" (370).

The ideal end result of detection and centralization in India would be the apprehension and swift execution of the Thugs. Upon conviction, Thugs would be hanged unless they turned King's evidence and participated in a host of new policing strategies: giving detailed confessions, naming names, working on stakeouts and lineups, and leading authorities to the grave sites. The reward for full confession was life in a Thug prison, like the one at Jubbulpore, where, due to the hereditary and absolute nature of Thuggee, mandatory celibacy was enforced (even of Thug descendants who had themselves never "tasted the goor") (James Sleeman 175–76). Thug crimes are represented as a hidden, widespread, and permanent part of the culture so that what was previously unacceptable as methods of English criminal justice— detection, centralization, and even arguably capital punishment—could be consistent with English national character and seen not as hidden measures but rather as an extension of public vigilance.

That the Thug Police became a model for future policing as well as a benchmark of good government in India is seen both in the subsequent success of "intelligence" work and in twentieth-century representations of the Thuggee and Dacoity Department. Subsequent campaigns against dacoity (gang robbery) and the criminal tribes legislation, for example, extended the Thug Police's ethnographic policing. Sir Percival Griffiths, in his history of the Indian police, suggests that "India can fairly claim to have been ahead of Britain in realizing the need for specialist organizations for the investigations of certain forms of crime"; all "modern organizations" of police intelligence, such as the Special Branch of the CID, "were a natural development from the new and expanded functions of the Thagi and Dakaiti Department" (342).[12] Indeed, an initially resisted detective arm of the Metropolitan Police was developed a few years after the victory over Thuggee, the same branch celebrated by Dickens (who was familiar with the work of Captain Taylor) as a delightful sign of the times.[13] Many twentieth-century historians also remember the Thug Police as a sign of proud imperial accomplishment. According to Brigadier General Horwood, a commissioner of the Police of the Metropolis, "of all the benefits which British Rule has brought to India the suppression of Thuggee must, to the Indian, constitute one of the most outstanding" (v). Griffiths's equally misty-eyed portrayal of the long-lived reputation of the Thug Police illustrates the endurance of this representation: "in the forties of the present century, the office of the Intelligence Bureau in Simla was known to rickshaw wallahs as the Thagi Daftar [office] and the memory of a great British success in suppressing an odious crime was thus kept alive in the speech of humble folk" (121).

Here, then, are the ideal English police as they emerge in accounts aimed to satisfy English curiosity newly engaged by a mysterious India. In the story that the Thuggee narratives attempt to tell, the police seize the opportunity of Indian criminality to restore a shaken faith in Empire, criminal justice, and England's character, while earning the trust of previously skeptical readers. And yet such strenuously urged "public vigilance" about a crime that took not even a single European life (with the notably arguable exception of Edwin Drood) suggests something else is going on.[14] The real interest here is English acceptance of what was then far from acceptable at home (policing) and what was far from certain abroad (the British government's public image as a benevolent authority).[15] The opportunity Thuggee provided reformers for addressing the identity crisis of the emergent police force suggests why this crime—which could be traced back to the reign of Akbar, was documented by the French traveler Thevenot as early as the seventeenth century, and was officially recognized by the British Army in 1810 (after it had lost a couple of sepoys to the practice)— was not "discovered" until this moment of reckoning for English law and order.

THE THUG POLICE

James Mill's instructions to Thomas Babbington Macaulay, whom he selected as legal member of the Supreme Counsel, were to establish "a general system of justice and police, and a code of laws common (as far as may be) to

the whole people of India" (Stokes 1959, 193).[16] Macaulay, aware of his
uphill climb, writes in "Notes on the Indian Penal Code," "It is clear that we
find the law in a state of utter uncertainty. It is equally clear that we cannot
leave it in that state" (265). Not only must there be better government,
Macaulay explains, but it must come to be associated with Englishness: "It is
natural and inevitable that in the minds of a people accustomed to be governed by Englishmen, the idea of an Englishman should be associated with
the idea of government" (227). William Sleeman, in advocating changes in
the Indian police system, is concerned with a potential gap between "our
power in India" and "the *justification of that power*" (1844, 2:454).[17] In an
1841 letter to his cousin, Taylor expresses a similar concern: "Crime in many
places increases rather than diminishes and in no case is the Police effectual
for the prevention of offences, many of them committed under their very
noses (1986, 31).

While the problems with the justice system were widely acknowledged,
Sleeman's cousin Henry H. Spry, explains that there are no easy answers:
"How far the civilized notions of English legislators have contributed to the
moral improvement of our benighted brethren in the East, although a question of great importance, and easily asked, is by no means so readily
answered" (1844, 2:150). Both the desirability and instability of this equation between Englishness and law and order is evident as these Thuggee narratives work to close that gap. As narratives that work to introduce the
detective and his story to a more receptive public, they represent difficulties
inherent in the production of authority. It is necessary to emphasize the crisis of English authority from which the Thug Police emerge, as recent readings of Thuggee narratives emphasize instead a sure-footed Benthamite
confidence at work in the Thug Police's methods.[18]

As often as not, these Thuggee narratives do not demonstrate confidence
but rather "confess" the instability inherent in the production of confidence.
Such instability marks the police reformers' deliberate transition away from
force and toward the moral authority necessary for public acceptance of the
police. As Philip Smith suggests about Victorian policing, "controlling police
violence and substituting moral force for physical force were necessary to win
public support" (116). The General Instructions issued to the new
Metropolitan Police in 1829 put restraint at the top of the list, "There is no
qualification more indispensable to a Police Officer, than a perfect command
of temper, never suffering himself to be moved in the slightest degree, by any
language or threats that may be used" (Stead 41). This was the climate abroad
as well. Both Sleeman and Macaulay were aware, as Trevelyan suggests here
about the suppression of Thuggee, that "the application of force can only be

a temporary and partial remedy" (394). The duties of the Thug Police, Hervey explains, "were of no ordinary character, and had to be persevered in and still carried on amid many difficulties, requiring both tact and temper to be contended with" (1:63).

The public relations challenges faced by the New Police are most apparent in the two policing strategies that brought down the Thugs: the death penalty and the use of confessions. The death penalty was given swiftly to any Thug whose confession did not yield subsequent and significant convictions of other Thugs. Midcentury estimates of the number of Thugs executed place the number at well over a thousand. However, for a country attempting to eliminate widespread use of the death penalty at home in order to embody a less "bloody" justice, this final solution for the Thugs presents an image problem. The swift use of the death penalty as well as the relaxation of the rules of evidence, discussed below, write British practices into a story of cultural violence that Thuggee seemed to tell only about Indian culture. As suppressing Thuggee was something the British claimed to be doing exclusively *for* India, it was also done entirely *to* India (no British perpetrators or victims), underscoring rather than exorcising the uncomfortable balance between coercion and consent that marked contemporary concerns about policing and imperial administration.

The most criticized aspect of the Thug Police's methods was its reliance on confession, a strategy that illustrates not only the police's credibility problem but the site of its potential resolution as well. Thug confessions challenged British standards of evidence. Sleeman addresses this issue directly, acknowledging that "the evidence of men whose preliminary step must be to confess themselves the most ruthless villains in existence, is naturally received with distrust" (1839, 61). W. O'Brien's article on the police system of London, admitting that "almost all [of the policeman's evidence]. . . . is obtained from the criminal population" (12), suggests that such tainted evidence is similarly the chief obstacle to the acceptance of investigative measures in England. The Thug Police's concern about the reliance on native confessions illustrates an uncertainty about British authority that is not often attributed to colonialist texts. Mary Louise Pratt suggests that the "conventions of travel and exploration writing constitute the European subject as a self-sufficient, monadic source of knowledge" who bears only traces of devalued non-European representation (136). But Sleeman and the other Thuggee chroniclers, far from self-sufficient as they are dependent on both dubious informants and doubting administrators, feel the need to clarify a process based almost entirely on at once highly valued and devalued "non-European representation." Sleeman is aware that "a prejudice has gone forth against the mode of conducting . . . the investigations" and thus provides the following meticulous explanation:

> The mode of proceeding is, to take the deposition of those who turn approvers, where this may happen to be. These men are then required to give . . . as full account of every expedition on which they have been, mentioning the dates of every one, and the detail of every murder; together with the names of those who had formed the gangs, their residence, caste, etc. etc. All this is registered in the office of the general-superintendent, and lists of those to be apprehended are sent to the different subordinate officers, who are all provided with approvers and guards. These officers also take the depositions in full of all whom they may apprehend, copies of which are sent to the general-superintendent. It is obvious that when depositions, thus taken almost simultaneously from different people hundreds of miles apart, who have had no means of collusion, and none of them expecting to be apprehended, agree in describing the same scenes and the same actors, it is obviously next to impossible to refuse belief. (1839, 69–70)

This elaborate demonstration of the Thug Police's system reveals how doubts about British justice help produce a need for the figure of the detective. While Sleeman argues that this system stabilizes both potential native treachery within the testimony and individual carelessness on the part of the British authorities, it is still fallible (it is only "*next to* impossible to refuse belief"). Since there will always be doubt, the information itself is less important than the interpreter himself. As Sleeman senses, the reader ultimately has only his word for it. But this is precisely the point. If the Thug Police's use of confession seems unstable because of native credibility problems and a loose application of British law, its legitimacy depends solely on the credibility of the interrogator, the English detective.

THE DETECTIVE AND HIS GENRE

We have seen how Sleeman, as a writer, publicizes his system of information gathering and thus diffuses fears of both spying and centralized policing— sites of public alienation from past policing. We have also seen how Sleeman, as an administrator, is adept at recognizing other potential sites of alienation from his work, such as the reliance on confessions. But it is as a character, as the literal hero of these Thuggee detective stories, that Sleeman answers the questions he himself and the other Thuggee texts raise about the nature of British authority. It becomes increasingly clear in midcentury accounts of police work, such as Dickens's celebration of Inspector Field, that the often precarious connection between "Englishness" and "law and order" is best figured not in abstract invocations of Law, but in an embodiment of the law. Sleeman was such a character.

While Sleeman did not work alone (he had a staff and was not even superintendent for his first years of Thug policing), he is represented everywhere as singular, as "that one man [who] rose from our midst" to fight crime (Hervey 74). He is the hero of almost every Thuggee text, always thanked in introductions, footnotes, and conclusions. Thornton writes of Sleeman in his introduction that it is "to the researches of that Gentleman, all writers on the subject, in common with the author of this volume, must be deeply indebted" (1). Sleeman is such a palpable figure in these narratives that he is always quoted rather than paraphrased. He is represented as the embodiment of the English virtues the reformers desired for the New Police, the first among which was sympathy.

Recognizing that the hardest battle to win in the post-Peterloo era was an association of the police with nonviolence, propolice reformers emphasized the police's capacity for sympathy, rather than for efficiency or order. An association between the New Police and the quality of sympathy was key not only to public acceptance of the police but to its new kind of police work, one based on centrally organized local knowledge. A sympathetic understanding of the men being interrogated could yield a much more useful type of local knowledge. This is evident in the writings of Sleeman, who has a sympathetic familiarity with native custom and language, which only makes him a more proficient policeman.

In order to address public distaste for spying, it is also crucial that Sleeman be visible. Reading these texts produces an uncanny sensation that Sleeman, like the mysterious crime he pursued, was everywhere. Far from embodying a kind of Foucauldian invisibility, Sleeman, instead of spying on criminals, is spied on by criminals. This reversal is evident in a representative anecdote recounted by Sleeman's daughter. Sleeman, sitting in an armchair in his study,

> suddenly had a premonition of evil, drew aside a curtain concealing an alcove, and disclosed an Indian standing there armed with a dagger. Unarmed as he was and not expecting such an attack, Sleeman had spent too much of his life in the midst of danger to be perturbed by anything like this, and, pointing a finger at the man, he said, "You are a Thug." The man promptly dropped the dagger and said, salaaming profoundly, "Yes, Sahib." The power of the human eye is said to be great, and many Thugs testify that Sleeman's had such a compelling force that they were obliged to tell the truth when under his cross-examination. (1933, 125–26)

While only an anecdote, many texts use the compelling glare as a synecdoche for Sleeman. Ameer Ali, the hero of Taylor's novel, describes a superintendent, who is believed to be modeled on Sleeman, as a "tall, noble-looking person he was, and from the severe glance he cast on me I thought my hour was come" (330). The unarmed but unshaken detective, whose "compelling force" is not a gun or a baton but the power of his eye and his wagging, knowing finger, is, to any reader of detective fiction, a familiar narrative type. In fact, how clearly he casts the mold for this type is evident in two of the most popular later benevolent authorities—Sherlock Holmes and Dickens's Inspector Bucket. Biographer Sir Francis Tuker describes Sleeman's face: "We notice . . . the large . . . omnivorous eyes, observant in seeking to understand, because wanting to act out a purpose. His intelligence . . . is brought alive by compassion" (2). If Sleeman has the sympathetic intelligence of a Bucket, he is the thinking, reasoning machine we associate with Holmes. According to Griffiths, "Sleeman's reports on the depredations of the Thugs are a model of objective reporting—calm, unemotional, factual accounts of episodes which were in reality highly dramatic. They typify the cold logical analysis which underlay his methods and which led to a remarkable degree of success within a decade" (132). James Sleeman describes his grandfather's work as "scientific deduction" (114).[19] That Sleeman's method and character met the criteria for popular acceptance is evident in O'Brien's mid-century description of the detective's "art" in the *Edinburgh Review:*

> In this art, success depends much upon individual qualifications, sagacity in drawing inference from slight things, fertility of resource, a blood-hound tenacity of pursuit, intimate acquaintance with the habits of thieves, and of their mode of acting in particular circumstances, and in the knack (and here genius displays itself) of making a *cast* in the right direction in search of a clue. (11–12)

Sleeman so embodied the good cop and his story was so "widely-extended" into the very heart of British imperial culture that even though he died in 1856 he played a role in *the* law-and-order crisis of British India: the Mutiny.[20] Sleeman was clearly a symbol for the type of order obviously lacking when the Residency at Lucknow was besieged. A portrait of the by then Major General Sleeman, K.C.B. hung on the wall at the Residency, from which the weary British residents escaped after five months; after he was safely out, Colonel Ouvrey of the 9th Lancers remembered the portrait and stole back into the residency, cut the canvas from the frame, rolled it around a soldier's musket, and carried it home to England. Real-life stories like this are a hard act for fiction to follow. And yet this anecdote, which begins Tuker's biography of Sleeman, illustrates how "real" events literally retrieve the story of the ideal English police invented in the representations of Thuggee.

Philip Meadows Taylor's *Confessions of a Thug* traverses this space between representation and invention and in so doing carves out of the diverse textual spaces of the other Thuggee narratives a new type of story. Taylor claims that this story of Ameer Ali, who killed almost seven hundred people (his name means "nobleman" and suggests his place as prince among Thugs), is "alas! Almost all true." In this "almost" we recognize that something is happening to facts that by themselves could not tell the whole story. Like Sleeman's information being "next to impossible" to disbelieve, thus making it absolutely necessary to believe in Sleeman himself, it is clear that a faith in the storyteller is the crucial question of Taylor's work. This is not always an easy question to resolve, as the novel is written by a British official and model administrator but told mostly from the perspective of an Indian criminal.

Nevertheless, Taylor was uniquely positioned to navigate this narrative terrain from detective work to detective story. "It was not until Philip Meadows Taylor's arrival on the English literary scene in the late 1830s," James Simmons writes, "that we find a man fully qualified by personal experience, an intimate knowledge of Indian customs and history, and a sympathetic rapport with the Indian people to write intelligently and accurately of the rich experience offered by the vast Indian subcontinent" (154).[21] Taylor explains the origins of *Confessions* in his autobiography: "I wrote and sent home to my father an article on Thuggee, which was shown to Sir Edward Bulwer, who sent me word that had he possessed any local knowledge of India or its people, he would write a romance on the subject; why did I not do so? I pondered over this advice, and hence my novel 'Confessions of a Thug'" (73). While he embraced Bulwer's idea, Taylor had strict rules for his romance. What there is of fiction in Taylor's "almost all true" tale "has been supplied," he explains in his introduction, "only to connect the events, and make the adventures of Ameer Ali as interesting as the nature of his horrible profession" (vii).

In "connecting these events" with an eye to awakening a potentially reluctant readership, Taylor provides the "one connected statement" of Thuggee that Trevelyan and others suggest is lacking in Sleeman's bulky account and, even more important, shows that the popular acceptance of the detective requires not propolice reformers' philosophical arguments but a story. Much as Sleeman was the "one central authority" for information about the Thugs, Taylor, as novelist, was able to give shape to the "hybrid textual activity" produced by the Thug Police's ethnographic methods and the diverse textual accounts of their operations.[22] As Sleeman made sense of a criminally chaotic India through his maps and glossaries, Taylor made sense of Sleeman's narrative chaos.[23] Taylor initially feared that he would always be in Sleeman's enormous shadow, but even during their lifetimes, Taylor's work was by far the more widely read. In a look at "the Secret Societies of Asia—the Assassins and Thugs," Frederick Holme uses Taylor's novel rather than Sleeman's *Ramaseeana* as the factual source for his claims.[24] Histories of the Indian Police tend to cite Taylor's novel, rather than Sleeman's tomes, as the reference work of choice on Thuggee.

Holme and the historians are by no means wrong to use the novel as a Thuggee compendium, in that the novel provides almost exactly the same account of the superstitions, omens, rituals, and practices of the Thugs as the work of Sleeman. As Ameer Ali tells of learning the craft from his adoptive Thug father, Taylor uses Thuggee as a map for exploring a wider range of Indian practices and beliefs. By following Ameer Ali's account of his life as a Thug, the reader is treated to a colorful picture of India, unrivaled until Kipling's Kimball O'Hara traveled the Grand Trunk road. Mixed in with accounts of such widespread Indian crime as homicidal tigers, torture, nefarious activities of the Dacoits and sundry criminal tribes are attentive descriptions of native festivals as well as a tour of the sites of numerous India cities, from the tombs of the kings of Goldonda to Hyderabad's Char Minar. Indeed, a contemporary reviewer writing in the *Literary Gazette* suggests that the authentic portrayal of India contained in this crime novel is its selling point: "the sketches of Oriental manners, customs, and society are alone a high recommendation to this publication. We know not when we have seen them better depicted" (468).

As Taylor's crime story, like the other Thuggee texts, is inseparable from a story about Indian culture as a whole, his work would seem to be part and parcel of the ethnographic ordering of India, described by David as a "pattern of incremental acquisition of knowledge" that reveals "a determined ambition to conquer (and thus control entirely) the colonized subject through acquiring complete knowledge of that subject" (135). Indeed, Taylor does represent India as a mystery investigated by an observant Englishman. However, the main narrator is the master Thug himself, Ameer Ali. The choice of the criminal as the main narrator, surprising as it is to any reader of late-century detective fiction, is a logical extension of the convention of the other Thuggee narratives to include firsthand testimony in their accounts. However, as Ameer Ali's testimony takes over practically the entire story, it is less contained and more open to interpretation than Sleeman's more overtly mastering narratives. Nevertheless, it has been argued that, far from demonstrating Indian agency, Ameer Ali's status as storyteller demonstrates total containment. Brantlinger describes Ameer Ali as a perfect subject of imperial panopticism (88). As Ameer Ali politely, indeed effusively, submits his story before the discreetly managerial presence of the Sahib, he is demonstrating the latter's complete and effortless control—a clear-cut case of the panopticism both Brantlinger and David describe. This is a case other critics have made, as well. "Taylor's novel," Robert Grant Williams argues, "hyperbolically anticipates later anthropological studies insofar as it allocates the respective roles of colonized and colonizer according to the hierarchical relationship between confessor and silent, omnipotent interlocutor" (487). Ameer Ali does spontaneously puff British criminal justice, as in this plea to his Sleemanesque arresting officer: "you English are praised for your justice, and long as that list of crimes I never before heard of, you will not deny me a fair hearing and the justice you give to thousands" (330). It is true that Ameer Ali's status as storyteller does not *necessarily* render the Sahib less powerful and that the coercion of arresting and imprisoning (not to mention hanging) the Thugs *is* effaced by the consensual scene of confession—Ameer Ali can come and go as he pleases, often taking as much as a week off between installments. Still, panopticism does not satisfactorily explain this text. Not only have the English been equally criticized as praised for their "justice," as we saw earlier in this chapter, but Ameer Ali's sycophantic plea to the officer is accompanied by his unrepentant denial of any crime "I never before heard of," suggesting the presence of at least one other story.

What is clear in Taylor's novel, as the Thuggee narratives' convention of first-person accounts becomes the monologue of a three-dimensional character, is the risk of shaping policing developments to a newly discovered crime while defining justice as the distinction between them. In *Confessions of a Thug*, Ameer Ali's in-depth look in the mirror of his criminality contains another reflection: the systematic methods of Thuggee and the methods for suppressing Thuggee are by design the same (i.e., it takes one to know one), while also needing to show—literally—a world of difference.

From the very beginning of the novel, Ameer Ali is conscious of recounting his story not as unthinkable, but as fundamentally intelligible to the British reader. Discussing the practice of Thuggee as a sport, he tells the Sahib, "How many of you English are passionately devoted to sporting. . . . you even risk your lives in its pursuit. How much higher game is a Thug's!" (2). Thugs claim a divine mandate for their actions. Ameer Ali laughingly tells the unenlightened Sahib, "Ah! . . . I can never persuade you that I was fully authorized to commit them, and only a humble instrument in the hands of Allah" (178). The British, too, represent themselves as instruments of God, an analogy Sleeman makes, perhaps unwittingly, when he explains that because Thuggee was "founded in the faith of religious *ordinance and dispensation* . . . nothing but the interposition, under Providence, of the supreme government . . . could possibly extirpate it" (1839, 108). The lifeblood of Thuggee, as for the Thug Police, is information. Thuggee requires information specialists, "sothas" or "inveiglers," who "skilled in the arts of deception . . . enter into conversation, and insinuate themselves by obsequious attentions into the confidence of travellers" (Wright 132). Ameer Ali considers his own work as an inveigler as one of the Fine Arts. "To my perception," he announces, "the whole art consists in having a smooth tongue in one's head" (258). However, his aesthetic distinctions are not limited to his own actions. He is a vibrant critic of the whole spectrum of violence India provides. During a lull in Thuggee activity, Ameer Ali travels with some Pindaris but is ultimately disgusted at their "thick-headed" penchant for violence rather than the Thug practice of "a little management and a few soft words" (235). With the Pindaris's method of reckless pillaging "order . . . was completely at an end" and Ameer Ali and his Thugs "had no inclination to join in the excesses," he explains, "for a Thug is not savage" (237).

While his account confirms the rampant criminality of India, his position as critic, as an almost scientific observer of local cultural practices, again holds a mirror up to the work the Thug Police and by extension English readers do. As the English relocate the story of their own violence onto the Thugs, Ameer Ali reinvents his own violence as necessary, indeed beneficial, in the context of widespread savagery. Ameer Ali describes a particular killing where his victims were not innocent travelers, but rather a bunch of bloodthirsty criminals, and suggests that the townspeople, upon finding the victims, "all agreed that a great benefit had been done by unknown agents" (135). Just as the English claim to do, Thugs here see themselves as doing something for rather than to India—and the Sahib does not contradict Ameer Ali's representation of events. Such native discrimination about murder complicates the necessary criteria being put into place by Macaulay, Sleeman, and ostensibly Taylor for evaluating when murder is a crime and when it is a punishment, when it introduces a better way of life (the Sahib's perspective) and when it preserves one (Ameer Ali's). The advice given to Ameer Ali by his Thug father is the same as that being given to those new officers of the Metropolitan Police: "Be firm, be courageous, be subtle, be faithful; more you need not" (17). The similarity between the methods of thieves and thief takers, to use turn-of-the-century terms, was a chief obstacle to public acceptance of the police in the early-nineteenth century, and Ameer Ali's story, in its invested compartmentalization of cultural violence, is too close for comfort. If the relatively silent Sahib were to speak, he might protest too much.

For a book dedicated to individuals "vigorously prosecuting those admirable measures for the suppression of Thuggee," then, Taylor demonstrates a strange sympathy for his creation, a tone commented on by the *Literary Gazette* reviewer: "[Thuggee] has been described to us so vividly as to impart a fearful sympathy and ardour even to our breasts in listening to the tale" (466). Taylor is not simply an unusually soft-hearted administrator. As we saw earlier, Sleeman's own strange sympathy for the Thugs enabled him to understand and ultimately master their system. Even Parks, upon witnessing the indifferent way in which executed Thugs met their death, suggests that the stoicism of "these wretches . . . had it been in a better cause . . . would have excited universal sympathy" (1:201). Like Mary Shelley's Romantic monster, Ameer Ali's freedom to tell his whole story rather than just the criminal highlights demonstrates his family values. While "these monsters," the *Literary Gazette* reviewer explains, "are influenced by a religious principle in the deliberate strangling of every victim they can inveigle within their snares . . . in the natural affections for their own parents, wives, brothers, sisters, children, and friends, they seem to feel the opposite emotions with equal strength and intensity" (466). "Have I not ever been a kind husband and a faithful friend?" Ameer Ali asks the Sahib:

> Did I not love my children and wife. . . . Where is the man existing who can say a word against Ameer Ali's honour? . . . Have I ever broken a social tie? . . . Even failed in my duty or my trust?" When the Thug defends himself, the Sahib does not attack the veracity of his claims, but rather reminds him that "seven hundred murder. . . . make a fearful balance against you. (178)

Ameer Ali is shown to have full entries on both sides of the balance sheet, and his almost childlike faith in the righteousness of his actions is not lost on the Sahib, who confesses:

> Although the mind would ordinarily reject sympathy with the joys or sorrows of a murderer like Ameer Ali, one so deeply stained with crime of the most revolting nature, yet for the moment I was moved to see, that after the lapse of nearly twenty years, by his account, the simple mention of the death of his favourite child could so much effect him, even to tears, and they were genuine. (214)

Taylor again pulls his punches about Ameer Ali's criminality as he has him commit the most horrid crime, killing his sister, while presenting it as an Oedipus-like tragedy: He does not know the victim is his sister until he sees an amulet identical to his around her lifeless neck.

Taylor's problematic prostration before the narrative powers and strange humanity of Ameer Ali illustrates the contemporary problem that motivated a new story about the police: When it comes down to two stories, that of the criminal and that of the detective, which can be trusted? Can the Sahib's relative silence in *Confessions of a Thug* be read as a tacit confession of a bad cop? In conclusion, I will suggest why Taylor, who as an administrator was entirely aware of the precarious police mission and their uphill climb toward acceptance, might have given center stage to the master Thug.

If the precarious position of this text stems from the inevitable sympathy the Sahib, as well as readers, feel for such a fully drawn character, it is a necessary risk. Taylor recognizes, as Sleeman and Macaulay did, that sympathy, rather than force, must be the battleground because it is *the only* battle that the militarily and economically superior British still need to win abroad—and indeed at home, as demonstrated by the public relations disaster of Peterloo. All of the writers of the Thuggee texts are aware of both the necessity for and the elusiveness of a *benevolent* authority, and this is precisely why the figure of the detective, passively engaged in the acquisition and ordering of knowledge, is so attractive. Indicating that English readers and writers are aware of the old story that the new, more sympathetic story of British justice replaces, Holme represents the suppression of Thuggee as the making of amends for the Bloody Code of earlier British "justice"; if under

> the vigilance of the British Government in India. . . . this monstrous hybrid of superstition and cruelty is destined to be finally eradicated, a title will thus be earned to the gratitude of the natives of India, which alone will make the benefits of our later administration more than atone for the injustice and rapacity which marked our early acquisitions of Indian territory. (244)

So important is this principle to Taylor's idea of Empire, it forms his last word in his autobiography:

> One word, one last reflection in regard to India, may not be out of place. It is to advise all who go there in whatever capacity, or whatever position they may hold,—use true courtesy to natives of all degrees. My experience has taught me that large masses of men are more easily led than driven, and that courtesy and kindness and firmness will gain many a point which, under a hard and haughty bearing, would prove unattainable. (464)

Spoken like the propolice reformers' ideal officer.

If the Sahib's sympathetic ear enables the Thug to justify himself, it simultaneously justifies the Sahib as someone given to sympathy rather than force. When the Sahib does interrupt Ameer Ali, it is to provide a moral, not a juridical clarity. For example, when Ameer Ali describes how he killed a man who offered him food, the Sahib exclaims, "And so you murdered the first man who had shown you any kindness after your misfortunes. Oh, Ameer Ali, you are indeed a villain" (303). When the Sahib hears Ameer Ali confess to a crime considered taboo even by Thugs, the killing of a woman, the Sahib cries "Wretch! . . . hadst thou no pity, no remorse, for one so young and so lovely?" Ameer Ali, confined, unlike the Sahib, by his immutable nature, simply responds, "I might have felt it Sahib, but . . . had I not eaten the goor of the Tuponee?" (201). Unlike the unrepentant Ameer Ali, the Sahib here employs the Thug's strategy of "a little management and a few soft words," as he represents a changed policing.

If this powerful English sympathy is the work of the New Police, then the work of the new detective story, represented by *Confessions of a Thug,* is to popularize this very story of moral ascendance over both criminals and criminal policing. This new narrative economy is driven by curiosity, not by force. The long-winded Ameer Ali fears that the Sahib has grown "tired of my minuteness" (197). The Sahib, who has earlier suggested that he grows "more and more interested in it," replies not with the command of a captor but with the weary encouragement of a captive audience, "No . . . I suppose you have some object in it, therefore go on" (197). Ameer Ali understands this new narrative strategy of using mystery to engage and detection to educate a distant and perhaps too-sluggish readership:

> I fear that I have often wearied you by the minute relation of my history; but I have told all, nor concealed from you one thought, one feeling, much less any act which at this distance of time I can remember. Possibly you may have recorded what may prove fearfully interesting to your friends. If it be so, your end is answered. (338)

Whatever concerns about the "Englishness" of the police that the Thuggee narratives assuaged for the Victorian reader, these narratives again unsettle for the critic. While the phenomenon of Thuggee afforded a reimagination of the English police, the imperial context of this invention requires that we reexamine both those histories of the gradual expansion of British police from the metropolitan center and accounts of British power abroad. The popular accounts of the Thug Police give a form both to an uncertain organization and to a genre here beginning to do what nineteenth-century detective fiction will continue to do: narrativize (not always confidently) the necessity of detection in an imperial world. But while former Police Commissioner Horwood rec-ognized this as a story that would be at home with detective fiction readers, writing that "this true record [of Thuggee] is of overwhelming interest . . . to others who, judging by the display of Detective Novels on Railway Bookstalls, are thrilled by works upon crime" (v–vi), not everyone has made the connection because of Thuggee's colonial context. These Thuggee narra-tives also require, then, that we reexamine the history of the detective narra-tive, seeing crucial developments in this emerging genre as originating in an imperial world, from darkest London to darkest Africa, understanding detec-tive narratives not as insular, ratiocinative puzzles, but as a genre that inter-prets many different, but all imperial, forms of writing for a British reading public.

The detective story aims to make the formerly foreign police into embod-iments of English values; in so doing, it must "discover" the detective and his story as a domestic product, a gradual and natural extension of English curiosity and characteristic vigilance, rather than the creation of an imperial culture. Hence, Inspector Field, Dickens's real-life symbol of the homegrown vigilance of the New Police and, as the model for Bucket, the figure largely taken to cast the mold for the English detective.[25] But when we imagine Field patrolling, as he would have, the exhibitions of the 1850s, perhaps passing the booth of Thugs from Jubbulpore prison that so delighted Victoria's son Bertie during an 1857 visit, we must recognize that the Indian murderers taken in by Field's compassionately omnivorous eyes are not the only imports.

❧ 3 ❧

MAKING AN ENGLISH
VIRTUE OF NECESSITY:
Dickens and Collins Bring It Home

I n "The Police System of London," W. O'Brien's 1852 article on the Metropolitan Police, the writer explains that

> even now, people do not always recollect that the only essential difference
> between a civil and a military body is the possession of arms: and that this,
> which constitutes the power of the soldier, destroys the usefulness of the con-
> stable,—for a soldier is necessarily a bad policeman. He cannot use his mus-
> ket by degrees. . . . Whereas the constable, because he possesses no deadly
> weapon, may safely be entrusted with the right of interference, and by a mod-
> erate application of force at an early period, may *prevent* the growth and
> progress of crime, which the soldier could only *punish*.[1] (10–11)

That this point—a soldier is a bad policeman—still has to be made twenty-
three years after the creation of the Metropolitan Police shows that the balance between "moderation" and "force" sought by early-century reformers is
not yet fully accepted by the public.[2] Not quite twenty years later, however,
the police are seen as preventive rather than punishing.[3] More importantly,
the police are not simply considered a necessary evil, but a representative of
what it means to be English.

The police baton, metonymically representing the police, also represents
this transformation. As O'Brien suggests, the difference between a punishing
soldier and a preventive policeman is their respective weapons: The soldier's
musket is deadly, the police baton is not. But what does a weapon do if it does
not punish? The police baton was a paradox from its inception, a symbol of

government authority imagined by a man who held that authority in contempt, Chartist radical Francis Place.[4] While the baton is defined above as "no deadly weapon," it is called "deadly" in Andrew Wynter's 1856 *Quarterly Review* article, "The Police and the Thieves," a contradiction that marks both a residual nervousness about the baton's (i.e., the police's) "offensive" nature and an emergent sense that what it represents is in the process of being defined. Wynter praises the policeman's "care . . . to hide his offensive weapon," while explaining that French police were "astonished at this forbearance: the Frenchmen could not understand why a man should carry a deadly weapon, unless to make a demonstration with it! In this little incident we see the essential difference between the French and the English character" (170–71). By 1870, neither the baton nor its meaning is concealed. An article in the same journal explains:

> The baton may be a very ineffective weapon of offence, but it is backed by the combined power of the Crown, the Government, and the Constituencies. Armed with it alone, the constable will usually be found ready, in obedience to orders, to face any mob, or brave any danger. The mob quails before the simple baton of the police officer, and flies before it, well knowing the moral as well as physical force of the Nation whose will, as embodied in law, it represents. (1870, 90–91)

Here the baton is both the arm of the police and the arm of the government and thus metonymically links two entities thought irreconcilable in the first half of the nineteenth century: the police and the English nation.

What happened in the 1850s and 1860s to transform the police into something that represented "the Nation"? The articles themselves provide a clue. O'Brien credits the recent "admirable descriptions in the 'Household Words'" for what little sympathetic understanding of the police then exists (12). The 1856 *Quarterly* article similarly praises Dickens's "excellent papers" on the Detective Police and even recounts one of his anecdotes. In arguing that the detective narratives of Charles Dickens and Wilkie Collins are central to what "happened" in the 1850s and 1860s to make an English virtue of the necessity of the police, I am both within traditional accounts of detective fiction and squarely at odds with them.

Most accounts of the emergence of the police and the detective narrative address the significant contributions of Dickens and Collins. Dickens's contemporaries credited him with having "discovered the modern detective" (qtd. in Philip Collins 196), a sentiment echoed in twentieth-century treatments of the genre.[5] T. S. Eliot's famous characterization of Collins's *The*

Moonstone as "the first and greatest of English detective novels" (464) has influentially posited Collins as the father of the modern detective and his genre.[6] Even those critics who do not see the arrival of the classic English detective story until Conan Doyle at least acknowledge Dickens and Collins as having provided important pit stops, such as plot twists, multiple narrators, and eccentric sleuths, on the seemingly inevitable road to Sherlock Holmes. Significantly, one of the innovations Dickens and Collins are credited with is the introduction of Empire into the genre; together they inaugurate a "tradition which set the English countryside crawling with Oriental assassins, Egyptian mummies, signs of four and the like" (Trodd xvii).[7]

In their often quite different representations of detectives, Dickens and Collins did both less and more than critics suggest. As Dickens and Collins are not showing up until the second half of this account of detective fiction as the explanatory genre of Empire, I am clearly not arguing that they provide the DNA for the genuine nineteenth-century English detective, nor that they introduce the Empire into the genre. For all the originality of their writings, Dickens and Collins do not invent but rather inherit the cultural debates on the nature of British authority and the national identity of detective work begun over half a century earlier. Such ongoing debate, of which the *Edinburgh* and *Quarterly* articles are examples, attempted to reconcile the at times violent authority the nation needed for law and order with the mild justice that was the very justification for an expansion of its authority at home and abroad. Well before Bucket and Cuff, these debates asked what kind of nation might the New Police come to represent and used the figure of the detective to explore possible answers. By the time Dickens and Collins are writing, then, earlier detective narratives have already established that Britain's expanding empire provided the conditions which made the police necessary, and that in creating the good cop, rather than the good soldier, England can demonstrate the "moral force" needed to legitimize its empire. These earlier narratives helped make sense of the Empire for English readers.

It is in their insistence that detective stories "make sense of England" and their representation of a resulting "imperial Englishness" that Dickens and Collins have the greatest influence on the detective genre and on the English reader.[8] Several years before Kipling would famously pose the question, the detective narratives of Dickens and Collins ask what do they know of England, who only England know?[9] The impact of imperial involvement on English character is the foreground rather than the background of their detective writings. Many critics argue that, to the contrary, detective fiction in general—and Dickens's and Collins's in particular—reduces the imperial and political into the domestic and personal. Mummies and moonstones are,

ultimately, only bits of not-so-local color. Hence the critical commonplace
that English detective fiction reduces the problems it presents, that it, as D.
A. Miller has influentially suggested, "performs a drastic simplification of
power" (69). Such readings articulate the logic of a particular version of
English nationalism as well, which divides the nineteenth-century imperial
imagination into a domestic core that was purely English and a colonial
periphery that was purely foreign. Dickens's and Collins's detective narratives,
often taken to provide just such exclusive reassurance about both the "homegrown" character of the genre and the nation, instead place the detective
squarely in the contact zone produced by Victorian imperialism.

The England of each author displays the messiness of a new imperial world
that makes the detective necessary. Rather than the English detective arriving
tidily and triumphantly as the imperial garbage man, however, his "necessity"
suggests a position that the public has regretfully endorsed. As O'Brien
explains regarding the public's attitude toward the rise of the New Police, "the
jealousy which watches such changes is slow in subsiding" (32). In different
ways, Dickens and Collins both attempt to make a virtue of this necessity by
reconciling the detective with English virtues. Dickens finds the English public within the detective, where Collins works to place the detective within the
English public. But Englishing the detective cannot erase the new imperial
world that his authority—and, I would argue, his very existence—signifies.
On the contrary, accepting the detective means understanding imperialism to
be a central part of English identity.[10] Precisely because their detectives connect English culture with Empire, then, Dickens and Collins bring the detective into English culture in a way that earlier writers could not. After Dickens
and Collins have written their influential detective stories, it is not the
English public but rather "the mob" that "quails before the simple baton of
the police officer." Their creations are, then, both formative and defining, but
not for the reasons traditional criticism would have us believe.

DICKENS AND IMPERIALISM'S NECESSARY DETECTIVE

Dickens's *The Mystery of Edwin Drood,* a story of orientalized, opium
den–hatched plots, which throws the shadows of violent mystery onto an
"ancient English Cathedral town," is both a story about imperialism and a
work of detective fiction. While the identity of "Datchery," the white-wigged
detective, who tantalizingly appears in the final installments, remains a mystery, it is clear that circa 1870, Dickens felt both that the "colonial question"
could be best characterized as a mystery and that the figure of the detective

was necessary for waking the novel from its nightmare of an empire out of control. But while *Drood* certainly documents the persistent imbrication of Empire and detection in Victorian culture, Dickens's writings in the early 1850s do far more to produce the detective as both a necessary imperial interpreter and a necessarily English figure than his more explicitly imperial foray into the detective genre. In his articles on the New Police, often dramatizations of expeditions the author took with detectives, Dickens addresses the issue at the center of the debates about the rise of the Empire and the police. If the writings of Godwin and James Mill, and the Thuggee narratives, were focused on the character of English law, Dickens sees the question as literally one of English character. Dickens newly emphasizes the *English* character of the detective as he makes him a familiar figure in his writings. In showing the English detective to be an agent of imperialism, his work during the 1850s, especially his journalism and *Bleak House,* shows Empire to be part of English identity.

Dickens wants the detective—both his work and his national identity—to be visible to the English reader. While the visibility of the detective in detective narratives might seem like an obvious point, it goes against both traditional and more recent readings of Dickens's detective narratives, which tend to ignore the history of the genre as a product of heated debates about the rise of the police and the Empire. Rather, critics have traditionally suggested that Dickens writes about detectives simply because he finds them so straightforwardly good. But it is because Dickens is aware of the exact nature of the problems his readers have with the police, such as their potential for violence and suspected foreignness, that he must make manifest the New Police's English virtues. More recent readings, such as D. A. Miller's enormously influential essay on *Bleak House,* argue that Dickens represents detection as panoptical invisibility. This has been a particularly persuasive reading because the fantasy of Dickens's writings, as I argue below, is of an orderly imperial world in which power would circulate so naturally as to be invisible. But to be satisfied with this reading is to ignore the more murky imperial reality that the very existence of such a fantasy suggests. It is a reality quite apparent in his detective writings.

Although his feelings about Empire figure prominently in Dickens's argument for detectives, it is not an easy task to situate him within Victorian discourses of imperialism. There are as many camps on Dickens's attitudes toward Empire as there are positions on imperialism itself.[11] The debate over Dickens's "imperialism" usually pits his vitriolic response to the 1857 Mutiny and the substantial—and substantially untroubled—presence of the Empire in his work against his critique of imperial concerns in the face of domestic social problems, for example *Bleak House*'s famous representation of the "homegrown" victims of "telescopic philanthropy." Dickens appears to speak directly to this debate in an essay on the ill-fated Niger Expedition when he warns real-life Jellybys: "The work at home must be completed thoroughly, or there is no hope abroad" (134). However, to make imperial involvement an either/or choice, as Dickens at first glance seems to be doing here, is to overlook that Dickens's imperial vision, like that of many Victorians, is myopic.[12] Reading Dickens's insular focus as the absence or opposite rather than the necessary complement of "imperialist feelings" replicates a cultural logic that attempted to preserve a particular national identity while working to generalize English civilization across the globe.[13] Part of the problem in assigning "imperialist feelings," particularly to Dickens, is that it is hard to tell where imperial concerns begin and domestic concerns end.[14]

A similar problem faced politicians as they assigned the first police jurisdictions. From their official inception in 1829, the Metropolitan Police had been prevented from operating in the City as a way of placating those police opponents worried about local autonomy. Police historian Clive Emsley suggests that such restrictions became problematic as the "Metropolitan Police performed 'imperial' tasks such as protecting the Queen, the royal palaces, Parliament and public buildings, as well as protecting society from the Fenian threat. . . . As the capital of a large empire the orderly government of London remained an 'imperial' rather than a local concern" (81). The imperial nature of domestic culture, and the confusion that results, is obvious as Dickens's "Metropolitan Protectives" perform their "imperial tasks."

For Dickens, then, as for most Victorians, to expand or not to expand is never the (only) question. The focus is instead on how to manage an expansion that has already blurred lines between imperial and domestic. Dickens's *fantasy* of imperial involvement is one of clear jurisdictions. He argues in "The Niger Expedition" that "the stone that is dropped into the ocean of ignorance at Exeter Hall, must make its widening circles, one beyond another, until they reach the negro's country in their natural expansion" (133). Dickens here attempts to balance "the home and the foreign works" through a concentric imperialism, which naturalizes the expansion of English authority as it places London at the center of an imperial world. And yet, what looks like an English insularity, a *center*edness, is also an expression of doubt about what the expanding modern nation is.[15] Dickens's city, "fog-bound and fever-haunted, brooding over its dark, mysterious river," G. M. Young suggests, registers the mid-Victorian conversion of London "into the imperial capital" (82). London and its empire are circuitously rather than concentrically connected. Dickens's fantasy of order is fogged in.

This is why detectives are necessary, and Dickens's New Police at once register this mysterious reality and represent the fantasy of an orderly imperial England. Philip Collins writes in his classic *Dickens and Crime* that Dickens's inability to "sympathize with established authority" has two "conspicuous exceptions": "the New Police and, overseas, . . . those who resolutely disciplined the turbulent native" (47). For Dickens, however, these figures are more or less the same exception, the same characterization of sympathetic authority. In short, the Dickensian detective is an agent of imperialism. The demands of being an imperial capital, Dickens suggests, make the potentially dangerous power of the police necessary. The detective returns the favor by making imperial power (its authoritarian implications and attendant threats of increased crime) safe for England. In order to make this argument, and to prevent the detective from backsliding into its earlier representation as a threatening "other," Dickens must complete the propolice reformers' mission of defining the detective as the upholder of national virtue. In making an English virtue of an imperial subject, Dickens also links Englishness to England's imperialist function.

A few years before Bucket, it is clear that Dickens figured out that the first step toward public acceptance of the detective would be to give him an English character. Dickens shepherds detectives into the national flock by twisting a typical antipolice argument that "the mass of the English people are their own trustworthy Police" (1868, 279) to suggest instead that the New Police embody the virtues of the English masses. A *Household Words* article, written by Henry G. Wreford, uses the Continental "spy police" as a foil for the English police:[16] The Secret Police system is "not merely a political institution, but [has] now become national. . . . I have seen it under all phases, and the effect has been to produce a want of faith in all that is high, generous and noble, and to form a low national character" (1850e, 613). As opposed to the victim of the spy police "across the Channel," the Englishman at home "has not the slightest fear" because "he knows that even if his fellow-passenger be a Sergeant Myth or an Inspector Wield, no harm will come to him" (1850e, 611).

Not only do English police value the English virtues of personal liberty and discretion; they marry these with a patient, familial benevolence. Two pages into Dickens's "The Detective Police," we know the detectives are "reserved and thoughtful," "well-spoken," "polite" men with "bright complexions" who do not interrupt their "brother officers." They more than observe the laws of human decency, getting a criminal his coat before taking him in, and scheming to get a murder suspect out of the sight of his devoted father before arresting him. Inspector Witchem modestly recounts a story about a famous horse stealer, Tally-ho Thompson, and reveals his own nonviolent, indeed friendly, methodology. Allowing Thompson a prebooking brandy, Witchem tells him, "I'm willing to behave as a man to you, if you are willing to behave as a man to me. Give me your word that you'll come peaceably along, and I don't want to handcuff you" (1850a, 367). Benevolence in Dickens is always linked to domestic comfort. When we first meet the detectives, they have been "most obliging" in accepting an offer into the "Sanctum Sanctorum of Household Words" (1850a, 358). Dickens feels comfortable letting these men into his home away from home, and he elsewhere represents policing as a homey, family business. He describes the station house at Wapping, formerly the Thames police office: "the old Court, with its cabin windows looking on the river, is a quaint charge-room: with nothing worse in it usually than a stuffed cat in a glass case, and a portrait, pleasant to behold, of a rare old Thames Police-officer, Mr. Superintendant Evans, now succeeded by his son" (1850b, 415).

By insisting on the New Police's Englishness, Dickens raises questions about what this identity means. In other words, the formerly foreign detective becomes newly English because there is something newly foreign about England. As Dickens floats "Down with the Tide" in 1853 with the Thames River Police, he experiences the river as an imperial hodgepodge:

> A very dark night it was, and bitter cold; the east wind blowing bleak, and bringing with it stinging particles from marsh, and moor, and fen—from the Great Desert and Old Egypt, maybe. Some of the component parts of the sharp-edged vapour that came flying up the Thames at London might be mummy dust, dry atoms from the Temple at Jerusalem, camels' footprint, crocodiles' hatching places, loosened grains of expression from the visages of blunt-nosed sphinxes, waifs and strays from caravans of turbaned merchants, vegetation from jungles, frozen snow from the Himalayas. (405)

In case the reader forgets where in the world he is after this list of peripheral particles, Dickens concludes, "Oh! It was very very dark upon the Thames, and it was bitter bitter cold" (405). The challenges of being an imperial city are particularly pronounced in the early 1850s when actual foreign bodies blew into London for the Great Exhibition.[17] The potential for "conspiracies of a comprehensive character" worried many Englishmen and stimulated Dickens's interest in an article on "The Metropolitan Protectives."[18] In a letter to W. H. Wills, his subeditor at *Household Words,* Dickens proposes their accompanying detectives on nighttime rounds: "It would make a wonderful good paper at a most appropriate time, when the back slums of London are going to be invaded by all sorts of strangers" (qtd. in Stone, 253). In the resulting article, London is the scene of distinctly international "mischief and confusion":

> A complicated web of machination is being spun—we have it on the authority of a noble peer—against the integrity of the Austrian Empire, at a small coffee-shop in Soho. Prussia is being menaced by twenty-four determined Poles and Honveds in the attics of a cheap *restaurateur* in the Haymarket. (Stone 254–55)

As he makes the detective seem English, Dickens makes England seem foreign. If England is foreign and the detective is English, however, this new figure for social order would be ill equipped to do his job, unless being English means being an imperialist as well.

Because modern London needs more than a town crier, the New Police must also be imperial explorers. Dickens's detectives have a global beat, evident in his depiction of the police at the Great Exhibition. He describes a rendezvous at St. Giles with a detective sergeant who is "weary of speaking French all day to foreigners unpacking at the Great Exhibition" (1850d, 389). Dickens gives this sergeant a multilingual ability not to hint at a kinship with the gendarmerie, but rather to show that the detective is in control of this new global London, center point of colonial wealth and destination of "foreigners." Thus the detective speaks French for the protection of England, though his fatigue reminds the reader that this is not the language with which he feels most at home.

That the English detective is an imperial explorer is best represented by Inspector Charles Field, who, Dickens explains in tones of awe, is "equally at home wherever we go" (1850d, 400). Dickens's descriptions of Field, a veteran detective and former Bow Street Runner believed to be a model for Bucket, make a point of reconciling familiar English virtue with global English authority. Inspector Field, making the rounds at an East End tenement with Dickens in tow, "is received with warmth *and* respect. Coiners and smashers droop before him; pickpockets defer to him; the gentle sex (not very gentle here) smile upon him" (1850d, 395). In "On Duty with Inspector Field," the eponymous detective is delayed from the aforementioned rendezvous because

> to-night, [he is] the guardian genius of the British Museum. He is bringing his shrewd eye to bear on every corner of its solitary galleries, before he reports "all right." Suspicious of the Elgin marbles, and not to be done by cat-faced Egyptian giants with their hands upon their knees, Inspector Field,

sagacious, vigilant, lamp in hand, throwing monstrous shadows on the wall
and ceilings, passes through the spacious rooms. If a mummy trembled in an
atom of its dusty covering, Inspector Field would say "Come out of that, Tom
Green. I know you!". (389)

Dickens shows Field having command over the spoils of colonial crimes as
well as local English criminals and—crucially—knowing the difference
between the two. Like the British Museum itself, Field interprets the objects
and, implicitly, the objectives of Empire, making them accessible, literally
safe, for the public. When Field finally joins Dickens he is shown having
come "from the Parrot Gods of the South Sea Islands, and from the birds and
beetles of the tropics, and from the Arts of Greece and Rome, and from the
Sculptures of Nineveh, and from the traces of an elder world, when these were
not" (1850d, 390). Guarding treasures of empires past, Field is both a symbol of England's imperial present (its "guardian genius") and a reminder that,
if not guarded by detectives, this present could end up in a museum with the
detritus of dead empires.

As Field walks his beat, then, he is both an agent of imperial fantasy and a
sign of the perilous imperial reality that makes him necessary. As his "duty" takes
him from the museum to his nightly patrol, he links an empire made familiar
and therefore safe, symbolized by a well-patrolled British Museum, with the
much more foreign world of darkest London. Dickens, accompanying Field,
wonders "how many people" would recognize "this compound of sickening
smells, these heaps of filth, these tumbling houses, with all their vile contents,
animate and inanimate, slimily overflowing into the black road" as "a not
remote part of the city in which their lives are passed?" (1850d, 390–91). In
these houses, specifically "Rat's Castle," Field is threading his way through an
urban Africa that he must domesticate. Dickens follows Field "through a
labyrinth of airless rooms, each man responding, like a wild beast, to the keep-
er who has tamed him, and who goes into his cage" (1850d, 401). The abject,
indeed animalistic, inhabitants are awed "before the power of the law, the
power of superior sense . . . and the power of a perfect mastery of their character" (1850d, 395). While Field is described as "the Sultan" of Rat's Castle, he
in fact demonstrates new English virtues of vast knowledge and restraint: He
knows everyone and collars no one. To make it clear that detection *is* an imperial methodology, Dickens describes the one in terms of the other:

To compare great things with small, suppose Leverrier or Adams informing
the public that from information he had received he had discovered a new
planet; or Columbus informing the public that from information he had

received, he had discovered a new continent; so the Detectives inform it that they have discovered a new fraud or an old offender, and the process is unknown. (1850a, 378)

Though he says he is comparing "great things with small," the effect of Dickens's comparison is to elevate the work of the detectives, rather than to deflate the discoveries of Leverrier, Adams, or Columbus.

In characterizing the detective as an imperial explorer, Dickens endorses the imperial fantasy that investigation is tantamount to management. An article written with Wills in *Household Words* describes the "incessant system of communication" of the New Police, which

> day and night, is kept up between every station of the force; we have seen, not only crime speedily detected, but distress quickly relieved. . . . We have seen that everything that occurs is written down, to be forwarded to head quarters; we have seen an extraordinary degree of patience habitually exercised in listening to prolix details, in relieving the kernal of a case from its almost impenetrable husk; we have seen how impossible it is for anything of a serious, of even an unusual, nature to happen without being reported. . . . We have seen that the whole system is well, intelligently, zealously worked. (Stone 273)

The beauty of this system, like the identical system employed by the Thug Police, is that it makes a virtue of the imperial necessity for inquiry; detection, the methodology of a well-run empire, relieves distress.

This fantasy of benevolent imperial authority is most fully realized in Inspector Bucket, and in saying this I am far from alone. Since D. A. Miller's influential essay "Discipline in Different Voices" most critics have read Bucket as an example par excellence of the power of liberal authority.[19] Indeed, Bucket's panopticism is as legendary in *Bleak House* criticism as it is in the world of *Bleak House*, and the connection with imperial policy has not gone any more unnoticed by Dickens's readers than by Dickens himself. Bucket indeed exemplifies the colonial observer in his "ability," in the words of Timothy Mitchell, "to see without being seen." Such an ability, Mitchell continues, "confirmed one's separation from the world, and constituted at the same time a position of power" (306). Bucket explicitly assumes this position as he rides during Tulkinghorn's funeral procession

> quiet among the undertakers and the equipages . . . Mr Bucket sits concealed in one of the inconsolable carriages, and at his ease surveys the crowd through

the lattice blinds. He has a keen eye for a crowd—as for what not?—and looking here and there, now from this side of the carriage, now from the other,
now up at the house windows, now along the people's heads, nothing escapes
him. (770)

But the reader sees Bucket if the crowd does not. And the importance of this
distinction is overlooked in recent readings of the novel. What makes the
dominant reading of Bucket's panoptical power unsatisfactory is precisely
that at the time Dickens is writing *Bleak House,* he does not want to confirm
the detective's "separation from the world." Dickens's energies are entirely in
the opposite direction, as he tries to depict these formerly un-English figures
as a national antidote for the uncertain English culture of the 1850s. To read
Bucket's power as panoptical is to hear only the first half of his motto. Like
Field, Bucket's refrain "I know you" demonstrates his power, but sensitive to
the uneasy implications of his knowledge, he gently adds "and you know me."

As Dickens creates and celebrates an imperialist subject position, he must
make of this necessity a visibly English virtue. Rather than rendering policing power invisible (Miller 17), then, Dickens must make a spectacle of the
English authority of imperialism's necessary detective. This is the purpose of
Bucket's trip to Tom-All-Alone's. As Field surveyed the mummies in the
British Museum, Bucket masters the "concourse of imprisoned demons"
(368) that is the otherworldly darkness at the heart of Chancery. Dickens's
description of Tom-All-Alone's is unmistakably taken from his first-hand
experiences on duty with Inspector Field:

> It is a black, dilapidated street, avoided by all decent people. . . . Now, these
> tumbling tenements contain, by night, a swarm of misery. As on the ruined
> human wretch, vermin parasites appear, so, these ruined shelters have bred a
> crowd of foul existence that crawls in and out of gaps in walls and boards.
> (272)

When Snagsby is mildly commanded to accompany Bucket to Tom-All-
Alone's, Dickens has the timid law stationer express the identical sense of
uncanniness he himself beheld when making the rounds with Field: "Mr
Snagsby passes along the middle of a villainous street . . . reeking with such
smells and sights that he, who has lived in London all his life, can scarce
believe his senses" (364). Bucket, however, is in control of these unnerving
surroundings, demonstrating the "thorough acquaintance with the geography
of their respective sections" that Smiles would admire in 1870 (101). So
familiar is Bucket with the population at Tom-All-Alone's that he instantly

notices who does not belong: "What are you doing here?" he asks. "You don't belong to London" (365). But rather than rousting the "vermin" from their hiding places, Bucket pauses, "not rough at all about it," to show concern for a newborn baby (366). Bucket emphasizes not the hustle of his work, but rather the "necessity of patience in our business" (799). Such an approach garners him the assistance of the inhabitants of Tom-All-Alone's. Resembling the respect with which Field is greeted at Rat's Castle, "the crowd flows round and from its squalid depths obsequious advice heaves up to Mr Bucket" (365) when he enters their territory in search of Jo.

My point that Dickens insists on the visibility rather than panoptical invisibility of Bucket's power may seem like a small one, but the implications are nevertheless large for a tradition of detective fiction criticism that has relegated the contested rise of the police and the Empire to the background. To allow Bucket's power to disappear in its guise as something else is to ignore the work Dickens has been doing to make the imperial combination of benevolence and authority an explicitly English virtue. It is to participate in the fantasy of traditional detective fiction criticism that the detective story is effortlessly English. Like the real-life detectives Dickens followed, Bucket, aiming "to make things pleasant," famously throws a cloak over George Rouncewell's handcuffed wrists. "I was mindful of your feelings when I come out, and I brought this on purpose. There!" Bucket exclaims as he literally cloaks authority with benevolence, "Who's the wiser?" (735). Because Dickens's earlier journalism has shown us the contact zone patrolled by imperialism's necessary detective, we are.

COLLINS AND DETECTIVE FICTION'S NECESSARY IMPERIALISM

While Wilkie Collins has been traditionally portrayed as a protégé of Dickens, deeply influenced by his writing, editing, and friendship, critical tradition regards the protégé as much more critical of social institutions than the master.[20] The most widely noted instance of Collins's independence from Dickens is their seeming difference of opinion about the ultimate midcentury exercise of British state power: the suppression of the 1857 Mutiny.[21] Dickens and Collins together represented the kind of "vexed responses" the Victorian public had to the Mutiny (Thomas 1993, 237). Collins "was much less aghast than Dickens" over the uprising, and though the former attempted to please the latter by contributing to a special Christmas Number of *Household Words* emphasizing English heroism in the face of mutiny, the resulting story, "The Perils of Certain English Prisoners," is hardly patriotic.[22] But if Collins was less comfortable with the virtue of authority than Dickens, his detective narratives, I would argue, actually go to greater lengths to render such authority acceptable to the English reader. The skeptical Collins does more than the celebratory Dickens to represent detective work and the detective narrative as *the* explanatory vehicle for a new imperial world and to cast the detective as a figure made both necessary and English by it. In so doing, Collins requires that we change the protocols of reading detective stories as domestic stories.

The question of how imperial expansion shapes the domestic world is central both to *The Moonstone* and to the criticism about it. The Verinder family's loyal retainer, Gabriel Betteredge, suspects as much when he wonders that in "an age of progress, and in a country which rejoices in the blessings of the British constitution" a "quiet English house" can be "suddenly invaded by a devilish Indian Diamond" (36–37). Dickens famously commented on the uncanny quality of Collins's novel in an 1867 letter to W. H. Wills.[23] "It is a very curious story," Dickens writes, "wild, and yet domestic." Indeed, Collins begins his detective story about a "quiet English house" with a narrative providing an eyewitness account of a violent crime committed by an Englishman during the storming of Seringapatam. More than a few critics have noted how *The Moonstone*'s prologue foregrounds imperial concerns, only to push these concerns aside with the profession: "what I write here about my cousin (unless some necessity should arise for making it public) is for the information of the family only" (6). In other words, Collins's novel ultimately reduces the wilderness of imperial politics to the far more manageable domestic problems of the Verinder family. What "begins as a violent military invasion," Ronald Thomas suggests, "gradually degenerates into nothing more than the unmasking of a spurned lover and an incorrigible chaser after women" (1993, 239). But such a position enables the "imaginary construct" that posits "empire and nation" as a "contradiction," and so denies "the formative nature of the colonial event in the domestic scene" (Gikandi 56). The family will with certainty ("necessity") become the larger family of the "public." What *The Moonstone* demonstrates is the necessity for an imperial interpretation of the novel's events. If Dickens locates English family values within the detective, then Collins shows how the figure of the detective necessarily draws the insular family—the Verinders and the English reader—into the larger world.

Similarly, what *The Moonstone* illustrates, as a definitive English detective novel, is that the tradition of detective fiction is by no means a domestic genre. Inheriting a tradition from such works as *Caleb Williams* and *Confessions of a Thug*, *The Moonstone* shares nineteenth-century detective fiction's two central concerns: (1) interpretations of the Empire for a formerly sluggish, now newly engaged (indeed, in Collins's terminology, "feverish") English reader and (2) the necessity for the English detective in an imperial culture. Such a reading challenges many critical beliefs about both this novel's and the genre's relationship to imperial concerns. In relation to the first point, critics have written abundantly on the imperial issues at the heart of the novel, but none of these otherwise important readings have linked the imperial issues to the work of detection that organizes the novel.[24] Indeed, the opening scene of imperial crime recedes in importance, critics would have it, precisely because the novel becomes a domestic crime story.[25] I argue that *The Moonstone* is able to remain a detective story, however, because knowledge imported from the imperial periphery keeps the investigation in play. In relation to the second point, D. A. Miller's influential reading of the novel argues that the text in fact demonstrates the lack of necessity for the professional detective. "The detective disappears . . . ," Miller writes, "and although he reappears to clear up some incidental matters at the end, the mystery is solved *without his doing*" (37). Because so many critics, like Miller, focus on what Cuff, the novel's professional detective, fails to do, it is important to recover what it is that Cuff actually does.[26] Cuff's ultimate return to the narrative is far from "incidental." While it might not signify his necessity for solving the literal investigation (an arguable point),[27] it shows his necessity to the story being told about detection itself and its evolving relationship to national identity in "an age of progress."

According to traditional readings of detective fiction, the story about detection that the detective story tells is one of the reduction of meaning. Anne Humphreys, comparing the detective novel to the more expansive "mysteries" genre, provides a classic description:

> In the detective novel . . . there is usually one central mystery and one detective. . . . The result of the detective's work is an affirmation of order and coherence. But the limited nature of the crime and its detection . . . also limits the potential for reading any large social significance into the solution of the "mystery". (457)

While this characterization does not fit *The Moonstone,* with its famous "team-effort" narration and multiple mysteries, nevertheless Miller's influential reading of the novel, which argues that there are many detectives, makes a similar case that "the novel is thoroughly *monological*" (54), that the many voices speak as one.[28]

The Moonstone is neither a story of one master sleuth nor of no master sleuth. Collins is writing at a time, and certainly about a time (the novel is set in the late 1840s) when the detective still occupies an unsettled and unsettling position in English culture. He therefore cannot stand above the culture nor disappear into it. Like Linda Colley's definition of nineteenth-century nationalism, in which commonality is superimposed on differences, *The Moonstone's* story about detection emphasizes the detective's necessary imbrication in the larger culture while insisting on preserving what makes him different: his specific expertise, which, we have seen, has become imperial in character. As in Dickens, such experts are necessary because the mysteries of Empire, in the words of the novel's lawyer, Bruff, "set all scrutiny at defiance" (311). And while "detective fever" does grip the nonexperts in the text, it is the *dialogical* relationship between the novel's experts and this newly engaged public that Collins emphasizes, not the latter replacing the former. For example, when Murthwaite, the celebrated imperial explorer, gives the inquiring Bruff two options—"Tell me . . . whether you will penetrate the Indian's motive for yourself? Or whether you wish me to save you the trouble of making any inquiry into it?" (315)—Bruff chooses both: He wants to do the detective work but needs Murthwaite's knowledge of the imperial periphery to proceed. Collins foregrounds the relationships between the "expert" detective figures with both the public and one another, rather than, as Miller suggests, "discard[s] the *role of the detective*" (42). The detective is required by the English reader to understand this new imperial world because a knowledge of this world has become necessary for the solution of English mysteries.[29]

Collins wastes no time making the case for the detective, showing the dawn of a new era of policing in, literally, the changing of the guard. Superintendent Seegrave, called first to the scene of the stolen diamond, is replaced by Cuff. In the few pages in which Seegrave appears, the "commanding" officer demonstrates "military . . . manners," a "military way," and a "military voice" (93,110,116). Just as O'Brien warned in the pages of the *Edinburgh Review,* Seegrave's militarism makes him a bad policeman: He alienates the repository of all domestic knowledge, Betteredge, by looking sharply at the servant's daughter with an eye that "was not a very pleasant eye to see" (99). "A more complete opposite to Superintendent Seegrave than Sergeant Cuff," Betteredge explains, "I defy you to discover, search where you may" (107). Cuff embodies the virtues reformers desired for the New Police: patience, sympathy, discretion. He meets abuse with forbearance because "in my line of life, if we were quick at taking offence, we shouldn't be worth salt to our porridge" (149). Though he does not "get many chances of exercising that virtue in my line of life" (126), Cuff is "tender to human infirmity" (126), looking out for the interests of Rosanna Spearman even as she seems to be a prime suspect. Sensing that he is "treading on delicate ground" (132) at the Verinder home, and emphasizing that he has a "reputation to lose" (180)—something that certainly distinguishes him from the old police—Cuff moderates his detective work with sympathetic understanding. As a New Policeman, Cuff does not have to sacrifice authority for sympathy. While his eyes are not militaristic, they are "immovable" (112). His voice is not authoritarian, "it was spoken very respectfully, but very firmly at the same time" (178). Collins demonstrates the difficulty inherent in such characterization; he describes Cuff's logic as having a "horrid clearness" and "an abominable justice" (184).

As with Inspector Field, these contradictory characteristics are made more palatable to the English reader by the detective's methodology: local knowledge. This type of detective work requires, as we saw in Dickens, sympathetic familiarity with the investigated and so neutralizes the potentially threatening work of detection. While Betteredge initially finds Cuff's method a "roundabout manner of going to work," it could not be more straightforward. Cuff's literal knowledge of English subjects enables him to mine, albeit carefully, English subjects for information. In conversation with the poor countrywoman, Mrs. Yolland, Cuff

> began with the Royal Family, the Primitive Methodists, and the price of fish; and he got from that (in his dismal, underground way) to the loss of the Moonstone, the spitefulness of our first housemaid, and the hard behaviour of the womenservants generally towards Rosanna Spearman. . . . In about a quarter of an hour from the time when we entered the kitchen, good Mrs. Yolland was persuaded that she was talking to Rosanna's best friend. (139)

Readers have pointed out that Cuff's knowledge, while extensive, is partial and therefore fallible. If Cuff sometimes loses, however, his method of detection—local knowledge—always wins. Cuff and Betteredge consult a local, "a man whose knowledge was to be relied on" (176), in deciphering the depths of the Shivering Sand. Jennings's personal knowledge of opium enables him to solve the mystery of Blake's sleepwalking. Murthwaite's specialized knowledge of Indian character provides crucial links in the story of the stolen diamond. When Cuff's lack of familiarity with Rachel's character leads him to suspect her, those with "special knowledge" of her character maintain her innocence. They are ultimately vindicated.

Miller would argue that the triumph of local knowledge represents the ascendance of generalized detection, rather than consolidation of that power in an agent of government. Conversely, critics intent on defining the genre of detective fiction focus on just this consolidation of "brilliant ratiocination [in] a mastermind to whom all the universe is, given half an hour, knowable"

(Trodd xv). These critics read detection as the work of superior individuals somehow set apart from the culture at large. Hence Cuff's "failure" in both these readings. What Collins is showing, however, is not failure but precisely the need for detectives to work within the larger culture. Cuff's initial limitations, as a sleuth and a suspect Englishman, force him to become part of the general culture, part of the "team-effort" that famously comprises Collins's novel (Trodd xv), while his special expertise keeps him from blending in. Cuff dramatizes the position of the detective in the mid-nineteenth century: As he balances English virtues of liberty and authority, he must similarly forge relationships with those figures who initially set themselves against him. This development is symbolized, to an almost ludicrous extent, by his love of roses, significantly the "white musk rose . . . our old English rose" (108). Cuff has a running debate with the Verinder's gardener about the best soil in which to grow the national flower, and in this debate the reader is shown a hybrid—"angel and devil by turns," to use Bucket's description of the detective—trying to graft himself onto the English nation.[30]

While Cuff's association with roses symbolizes the detective's implantation in English culture, the real work of grafting the detective to the nation is accomplished as Collins gives him an English everyman as an interpreter, inaugurating a crucial aspect of the emerging genre. Cuff befriends Betteredge, who becomes a Watson to his Holmes. According to John Cawelti, the Watsonian narrator, "a standard feature of the classical detective story," is important because he provides a "perspective and commentary on the detective's activity" (83–84). Through Betteredge, the work of detection and the evolution of English authority are explained to the reader. The symbol of "English common sense" (Taylor 202), Betteredge is the self-described "medium of introduction" (143) between Cuff and the common Englishman.[31] The Verinder's devoted family retainer has the most direct relationship to the reader in addition to the most pages of narration; he often begs to "excuse the faults of this composition," faults that stem from "my talking so much of myself, and being too familiar, I am afraid, with you" (213). Betteredge's familiarity with the common Englishman—his local knowledge—is precisely why Cuff deputizes him. Cuff explains his position to Lady Verinder: "I felt that a person of Mr. Betteredge's character and position in this house—knowing the servants as he did, and having the honour of the family at heart—would be safer to take as an assistant than any other person whom I could lay my hand on" (187). The local knowledge of the average Englishman, then, supports but does not supplant the detective's work.

As the detective needs the common man to understand a new mystery, Collins argues, the common man needs the detective to understand the mysterious new world in which he already lives. In the character of Betteredge, Collins dramatizes an Englishman's evolution from suspicion to appreciation of what Cuff represents: a complex imperial world and the profession (detection) such a world makes necessary. While some critics see Betteredge as an example of pure Podsnappery, the condition of Betteredge, like the condition of England, is changing as he is caught between past loyalties and present mysteries.[32] Betteredge's ties to English tradition are best revealed by his twin devotions to *Robinson Crusoe*, the urtext of British imperialism, and to Lady Verinder, "a mistress to serve . . . in ten thousand" (119). And yet, this loyal servant also represents a new public in a new era. Though the novel is set in the late 1840s, it was written during the debates over the Second Reform Bill. So while Betteredge is loyal to the family and to the duties of his position, he frequently casts his own vote, evident in his ambivalence toward several characters: Blake, whom he both serves and satirizes; Jennings, whom he tells that he will do anything he is ordered to, but makes it abundantly clear how these orders conflict with his own proper sensibilities; and Cuff, of whom he says, "I couldn't help liking the Sergeant—though I hated him all the time" (200). Betteredge's famous "detective fever" is a symptom of his transition. Betteredge gives into both his curiosity and his affections for Cuff as he learns, along with the English reader, that the world is not local, not controllable by the authorities of the past: Lady Verinder dies suddenly in the first half of the text as the apparently bloodless empire building of *Robinson Crusoe* is replaced by the violence of nineteenth-century imperialism.

In this new world, Collins asserts, the marginal figure of the detective has moved to the center of English culture. But rather than providing a tidy barrier between center and margin—between quiet English houses and devilish Indian diamonds—the detective illustrates that Empire is already part of English culture. Collins demonstrates this by linking the detective with a character almost always ignored in readings of the novel: Murthwaite, the celebrated explorer of the wilds of India. Where Dickens's New Policeman is characterized as an imperial explorer, Collins's imperial explorer is characterized as a New Policeman. Murthwaite is so substantially similar to Cuff that the knowing reader of detective fiction might raise an eyebrow at the fact that the two never appear together in the text. Both the celebrated detective and the celebrated traveler are famous nationwide. Murthwaite, like Cuff, displays the characteristics of the already established detective type. He has a "steady, attentive eye" and a "cool immovable way" (73). Murthwaite is similarly "not an easy man to astonish" (314). He displays a protean mobility; he sneaks up on the Indian performers unseen and withdraws "as quietly as he approached" (78). Not only does Murthwaite look like a detective, he acts like one. Blake seeks him out, feeling "bound . . . to tell you something which may possibly put the clue into your hands" (80). Cuff knows he needs to consult Murthwaite to further his investigation. After their (offstage) meeting, Cuff suggests they are of one mind about the Indian travelers: "there isn't a doubt on my mind, and there isn't a doubt on Mr. Murthwaite's mind, that they came to this place to steal the Moonstone" (165). In Cuff's absence, he serves as a consulting detective, and often a literal interpreter. Murthwaite's "long experience" with "the Indians and their language" makes him a valuable resource (152). Bruff is the Betteredge to Murthwaite's Cuff, trusting him "to lead me blindfold through the last windings of the labyrinth, along which he had guided me thus far" (321).

Murthwaite's otherness—he is described as "long, lean, wiry, brown, silent" (73)—would seem to underscore his peripheral value to the text and thus be a perfect example of the ultimate silencing of the imperial story by the domestic story. In characterizing Murthwaite as a detective, however, Collins asserts both that an agent of Empire is an English figure and that detective work, privately undertaken for an English family, requires a mastery of information about the imperial world. Murthwaite's "superior knowledge of the Indian character" (319) enables him to know what it means to be English, evident in his summary of the Indians' performance at Rachel's party:

> The clairvoyance in this case is simply a development of the romantic side of the Indian character. It would be a refreshment and an encouragement to those men—quite inconceivable, I grant you, to the English mind—to surround their wearisome and perilous errand in this country with a certain halo of the marvellous and the supernatural. (317)

Murthwaite demonstrates the detective's unromantic "English mind" in his suggestion that the troublesome diamond be sent off to Amsterdam to be cut up. Sounding like one of Dickens's detectives, he articulates his deductive process, in contrast to the Indian method:

> we have nothing whatever to do with clairvoyance, or with mesmerism, or with anything else that is hard of belief to a practical man, in the inquiry that we are now pursuing. My object in following the Indian plot, step by step, is to trace results back, by rational means, to natural causes. (317–18)

If we persist in reading Murthwaite as we have read Cuff, as colorful but limited characters who ultimately retire to the periphery (to the Indian and English countrysides respectively), we miss seeing how Collins makes an imperial story central to a domestic story. In making an agent of Empire a detective and making a detective part of the English family, Collins's novel suggests that imperialism is central to being English. While the ending of *The Moonstone* contains marriages, inheritances, and babies—the traditional conclusions of domestic novels—Collins has Cuff and Murthwaite conclude the novel, writing in from their distant locales to report on the exodus of the Moonstone from England to its original Indian home. Ignoring these missives in order to focus on domestic resolution would be akin to overlooking St. John River's inscrutable letter from India at the end of *Jane Eyre* so that Jane and Rochester's strange and wonderful domesticity would be the novel's parting image.

Nineteenth-century reformers promised in their accounts of the un-English police and the rapacious British Empire at the turn of the century that what began as signs of violent English authority could become symbols of triumphant English liberty. As weapons could become preventive rather than punishing, things that threatened the nation could come to defend it. In choosing a composite detective/explorer to solve the mystery of *The Moonstone*, Collins makes the same point. What begins as a violent failure of military order (from Seringapatam to Sergeant Seegrave) can become a triumph of local knowledge. By the end of the novel, English authority rests in the hands of good imperial detectives rather than bad imperial soldiers. This resolution does offer a narrative tidiness, but not, as critics have suggested, because of the work of a single mastermind or of the disappearance of troublesome imperial issues. As Collins, like Dickens, links the detective with the explorer and makes this imperial figure one to whom the English reader can relate, he suggests that the mystery of what it means to be English "in an age of progress" must be solved from the outside.[33]

⚜4⚜

SEPARATED AT BIRTH:
Doyle, Kipling, and the Partition of
English Detective Fiction

In 1887, Kipling introduced his fictional detective Strickland in the pages of the Lahore *Civil and Military Gazette:*

> [Strickland] held the extraordinary theory that a Policeman in India should try to know as much about the natives as the natives themselves. Now, in the whole of Upper India, there is only one man who can pass for Hindu or Mahommedan, hide-dresser or priest, as he pleases. He is feared and respected by the natives from the Ghor Kathri to the Jamma Musjib; and he is supposed to have the gift of invisibility and executive control over many Devils. But this has done him no good in the eyes of the Indian government. (1987, 51)[1]

Strickland's expertise in native life enables him to solve a range of mysteries from "the great Nasiban Murder Case" to a deadly curse ("The Mark of the Beast") to his own romantic entanglement ("Miss Youghal's *Sais*"). But while Strickland "knew too much," Kipling tells us that his name "is almost unknown to Englishmen."[2] And because Kipling wrote only a handful of Strickland stories, his name is almost unknown in literary tradition, as well. This character, however, is widely known under a different name: Sherlock Holmes.

Kipling's Strickland and Doyle's detective, who also appeared on the scene in 1887, are strikingly similar figures and not only for the qualities evident in the above passage, such as an encyclopedic knowledge of his environment and a gift for disguise. These characters have a more profound similarity: Their extraordinary and often misunderstood detective work reimagines national authority and thus the nation itself.[3] I say misunderstood because how these figures serve authority has received much more critical attention than how they have redefined it. Both Strickland and Holmes, for example, chafe against social boundaries as much as they defend them. Kipling explains that Strickland's exceptional detective work "has done him no good in the eyes of the Indian government," nor with the Anglo-Indian community: "people did not understand him. So they said he was a doubtful sort of man and passed by on the other side" (1987, 51). Holmes's "outré" qualities, from his cocaine addiction to his bohemian aestheticism, have been widely documented, as have his periodic departures from the letter of the law. Holmes frequently breaks the law in order to solve a case and seems at times a law unto himself; "I am the last court of appeal" he says on more than one occasion. Both Strickland and Holmes embody an interrogation of the character of English authority in the context of imperialism that shapes them as detectives and had shaped the genre of detective fiction for over a century before their simultaneous arrival on the pages of English fiction.

Why is it important that Doyle and Kipling create such similar characters at precisely the same historical moment? Because traditional criticism has used the work of Doyle and Kipling to partition, at this very same moment, detective fiction from spy fiction. Since Kipling presumably focuses on detection in the colonial world and Doyle on detection in England, it has been easy—indeed, too easy—to separate their work and see them as inaugurating distinct traditions: spy and detective respectively. It is the point of this book to show how difficult it was, throughout the course of the nineteenth century, to maintain the distinction between center and periphery. When literary criticism comes along and does what neither detective fiction nor stories of imperial intrigue were ever quite able to accomplish, it is understandably difficult for us to see how the two in fact collaborated to make understanding the interpenetration of core and periphery essential to the integrity of the nation. It is an interpenetration, I contend, which made the detective so necessary in the first place.

To say that the works and the worlds of Kipling and Doyle can be partitioned from one another seems shockingly inaccurate. Any reader knows that, from the Great Game at the heart of *Kim* to the Mutiny story at the heart of *The Sign of the Four*, investigation is as central to Kipling as imperial intrigue is to Doyle. Indeed, it has not gone unnoticed in recent criticism, to say the least, that Kipling's empire is shaped by a fantasy of surveillance (embodied by Strickland's successors, *Kim*'s Kimball O'Hara and Colonel Creighton) and that Doyle's detective is deeply involved in both the incidents and ideology of

Empire.⁴ But this recent critical attention to Kipling and Doyle when they travel across each other's geo-literary boundaries has not served to question these
boundaries. Rather, it reinforces assumptions about what divides them in the
first place: that they write from and about fundamentally different places. For
example, Jon Thompson, whose *Fiction, Crime, and Empire* importantly challenges "rigid generic categories" as a basis for literary analysis, nevertheless
employs these categories in a discussion of Kipling and Doyle.⁵ For Thompson
and many other critics, Kipling writes about Empire and thus writes adventure
or spy fiction, notably *Kim,* the "greatest of all spy novels" (Winks 1). Whereas
Doyle, because "the solitary detective's talents were incongruent with the scale
of international relations" (Claussen 123), writes about domestic problems and
thus writes detective fiction.⁶

On closer examination, however, the logic for such distinctions becomes
vague. Julian Symons, in a standard account of crime fiction, does not know
exactly what "the lines of demarcation are" between spy fiction and detective
fiction, "but everybody recognizes their existence" (214).⁷ Michael Holquist
can define the detective story only in terms of what it excludes: "a detective
story should be mainly occupied with detecting, which would exclude Gothic
romances, psychological studies of criminals, and hard-boiled thrillers" (154).
Ian Ousby reads "a decline in quality" in the later Holmes stories because they
have stepped outside of his traditional understanding of the boundaries of
detective fiction and into the stuff of espionage or adventure fiction. And
while he is forced to admit that this is not true across the board—the late story
"Thor Bridge" "compares favorably with the best of Doyle's work")—on the
whole, Ousby argues, these stories demonstrate "a cruder sense of the exotic
and macabre" (170). Ignoring that Holmes's concerns have always concerned
the "exotic" and needing to prove his larger thesis that Holmes is the classic
Victorian hero, Ousby provocatively concludes that the later Holmes has
"outlived his proper era" (170–72).⁸

As I have suggested throughout this book, the generic divisions sketched
here overlook and, more to the point, obscure the long history of the detective
as a primary agent in the Englishing of imperial authority. In so doing, literary
criticism has participated in the fantasy of Victorian nationalism that there are
clear distinctions between what is domestic and what is international, what is
central and what is peripheral.⁹ Gikandi describes how a "strategic forgetfulness"
enables such an elision of the colonial from what it means to be English (86).
The clearest example of this "strategic forgetfulness" at work in the treatment
of detective fiction is the oath of the Detection Club of London, formed in 1930
by Dorothy Sayers and fellow British mystery writers. Showing where critics
such as Ousby get their distaste for Holmes's un-Holmeslike, *unheimlich* devo-

lution into the exotic, members pledged "to observe a seemly moderation in the use of Gangs, conspiracies, Death Rays, Ghosts, Hypnotism, trapdoors, Chinamen." Here writers are encouraged to emphasize a homegrown rationality that, Dorothy Sayers explains elsewhere, assumes "a knowable universe" (Winks 101).[10] While not commenting directly on the Detection Club oath, W. H. Auden shows that the Golden Age of detective fiction *is* a fantasy in his argument that readers of this era of detective fiction are seeking to "be restored to the Garden of Eden" (Winks 24). Clearly, Golden Age writers and subsequent literary critics want to get back to some Edenic version of prewar England untouched by the "unseemly" and immoderate aspects of imperial rule—the stuff, now, of spy fiction. Golden Age detective writers want to reinvent themselves as the progeny of a prelapsarian Sherlock Holmes.

The group amnesia demonstrated in the Detection Club oath has found support in the strangest of places. One would expect an inattention to imperial matters in those treatments of the genre that see detective fiction as a parlor game or psychological puzzle.[11] But in influential accounts of detective fiction from Marxists to Foucauldians, detective fiction is characterized as serving exactly this same purpose of reducing meaning, whether it be exonerating society of crimes, simplifying the operations of power, or narrowing what it means to be English.[12] Jon Thompson suggests that it is the spy genre, not detective fiction, which has such broader concerns as "assert[ing] the necessity of covert, essentially undemocratic activities in the name of state security" (94). What such a definition covers up is how the figure of the necessary detective attempts over a long nineteenth century to balance the ideals of democracy with the need for state security. It is a balance that converts the detective from a suspicious turn-of-the-century "spy" to an imperial hero, such as Holmes. As this figure strives to reconcile the very different principles of democracy and national security, he is far less a sure-footed symbol of a knowable universe than a sign of a universe reimagining itself in an unknowable and often violent imperial age. Given the tendency of critics to read the detective genre as essentially conservative, I cannot stress enough the importance of the detective narrative's relation to a *liberal* critique of imperialism's "things as they are," to recall the original title of *Caleb Williams*. This is far from arguing that detective fiction is critical of imperial ideology. But detective fiction works toward public acceptance of authority and even solidifies imperial position not because of a wholesale endorsement of power but because it reimagines authority as consistent with, rather than an alternative to, milder liberal principles. The detective acquires cultural credibility precisely because he is seen to take into account common concerns about the abuse of authority at home and abroad.

What both the oath and much detective fiction criticism have done, then, is to dissociate detective fiction from its history. It is a history that contains magistrate Patrick Colquhoun's early-century analysis of the imperial origin of metropolitan crime, Edmund Burke's attempt to prosecute imperial crime in the person of Warren Hastings, and "Thuggee" Sleeman's/Captain Taylor's arguments that detective work is the work of Empire. I have hoped to show how critical tradition has ignored the contentious debates across the political spectrum in which crime and Empire cannot be understood without one another. Such debates make *Caleb Williams* an imperial novel as well as a detective novel and James Mill's *The History of British India* a detective story as well as a history of imperial mismanagement. These debates about the character of English authority in an age of Empire require that Dickens's and Collins's inspectors become colonial explorers and that colonial explorers/administrators, such as *The Moonstone*'s Murthwaite or Thuggee Sleeman, become detectives. In tracing the continuities rather than the distinctions between detection in the work of Kipling and of Doyle, I hope to show here how detective fiction makes imperialism central to what it means to be English rather than casts it from the garden.

BROTHERS

Find the answer to all these questions, and you will have done good
service for your country.
—Mycroft Holmes to his brother Sherlock in "The Adventure of The
Bruce-Partington Plans"

I begin with this quotation from Doyle's "The Adventure of The Bruce-Partington Plans" (1908) because that Holmes story, perhaps more than any other, best demonstrates my argument about the perils of generic partition. Not only does this story illustrate that the concerns of detective fiction are those we have retroactively assigned to spy fiction, but the story itself is a critique of the compartmentalization of foreign and domestic knowledge. Doyle gives a preview of the story's lesson about the necessity of integrating knowledge by beginning with Holmes, fogged in at Baker Street, "cross-indexing his huge book of references" (1994d, 37). The catalyst for the story's action is the theft of the plans for the Bruce-Partington submarine, technology so superior that "naval warfare becomes impossible within the radius" of its operation (42). Only part of the plans have been found on the discarded body of a junior government clerk, who, it would seem, had been selling state secrets. "It's a vital international problem that you have to solve," Mycroft tells his brother, Sherlock, as he pays a visit to the great detective at his Baker Street home (43).

Here we have it: a spy story in the middle of a collection of detective stories.[13] It would be easy to read this as spy fiction making a house call to the domicile of detective fiction, much as Mycroft, a government agent involved in international intrigue—"he *is* the British Government" (1994d, 39)—visits Sherlock, a consulting detective focused on the seemingly more narrow world of metropolitan crime. But in this and other stories, Doyle quietly but persistently critiques a distinction between the brothers' fields of operation. Despite the fact that his intelligence is characterized as being superior to that of Sherlock ("The Greek Interpreter"), elder brother Mycroft lacks the ability to solve the mystery of the missing plans alone. "Why do you not solve it yourself," Sherlock asks. "You can see as far as I" (43). The problem is that the kind of surveillance enabled by distance is not sufficient here. Accordingly, Mycroft persuades Sherlock that the fate of the nation depends on his inside, on-the-spot local knowledge: "But it is a question of getting details" (43). Mycroft may appear, in making this appeal, to be making an exception to his usual practice—his visits to Baker Street are rare. The successful outcome of this story suggests, however, that no one form of knowledge can exercise authority all by itself. To have power, one must effect a union or, in the words of Doyle, a "cross-indexing" of domestic and foreign knowledge. While Mycroft's "specialism is omniscience" (39), he lacks the authority of omniscience without Sherlock's "details." The mysteries of the modern world, as Doyle implies, can only be penetrated and, even more important, the chinks in the armor of state security can only be fixed if local knowledge and global knowledge are cross-indexed.[14] To underscore the mutual dependency of the two forms of knowledge personified in the brothers Holmes, Doyle attributes the international crisis that they must resolve in this story to the betrayal of one brother, Sir James Walter, by another, Colonel Valentine. This story begins with the comprehensive activity of "cross-indexing" and emphasizes the importance of two carefully distinguished but (literally) related parts working as one. Doyle drives the point home by ending with Holmes returning to his monograph upon "polyphonic motets," a type of choral composition in which two or more independent melodies are juxtaposed in harmony.[15]

This story of two brothers provides a road map for my reading of another set of related writers whose work has been wrongly separated: Kipling and Doyle. Rudyard Kipling's 1901 novel, *Kim,* is arguably the definitive novel about the Great Game of turn-of-the-century imperialism and the novel's title character the embodiment of the Game. The Holmes stories, however, are about the Great Game as well, and its rules shape the Great Detective as they do Kimball O'Hara. Kipling's and Doyle's detectives play the Game for similar reasons. (I will consider all Kipling's "detectives," Strickland, Kim, and Creighton, in the subsequent discussion.) Playing the Game invigorates Kim: "Kim warmed to the game. . . . the sheer excitement and the sense of power. He drew a new breath and went on" (95). Holmes is similarly characterized as literally coming to life when solving a mystery:

> See the foxhound with hanging ears and drooping tail as it lolls about the kennels, and compare it with the same hound as, with gleaming eyes and straining muscles, it runs upon a breast-high scent—such was the change in Holmes since the morning. He was a different man to the limp and lounging figure in the mouse-coloured dressing-gown . . . only a few hours before. (1994a, 48)

As these detectives breathe the Game, it is—almost—their whole lives. Kim's playing of the Game is paralleled in the story by "the Way." In describing the Way, Kim's beloved lama also describes the rules of the Game: "But those who follow the Way must permit not the fire of any desire or attachment, for that is all Illusion" (140). And indeed Kim does play the game with increasing professional focus throughout the novel. But he does have an attachment in addition to the game: the lama, who is, Kim says, "one part of my bond." As with Kim, Holmes lets nothing distract him from the Game:

> All emotions . . . were abhorrent to his cold, precise, but admirably balanced mind. . . . They were admirable things for the observer—excellent for drawing the veil from men's motives and actions. But for the trained reasoner to admit such intrusions in to his own delicate and finely adjusted temperament was to introduce a distracting factor which might throw a doubt upon all his mental results. (1977, 1)

Again, as with Kim, this professional intensity is true of Holmes with one exception: Watson. The good doctor and war veteran is hardly lamaistic—he is the voice of English pragmatism. But Watson and the lama serve as characters through whom the detective figure can himself be investigated and therefore made familiar. Not only is this a crucial move, as I have argued throughout this volume, in order to bring a figure formerly feared as foreign into the fold, it also requires that the detective's focus be extended to include the experiences of Empire, whether that be the lama's quest for eternal life or Watson's experience in the Afghan campaign.

Kim and Holmes are similar in both their stated and more serious reasons for playing the game. What Kim "loved was the game for its own sake" (51). Eight years later, Holmes will tell Mycroft that he is not interested in titles as a reward for solving important matters of state: "I play the game for the game's own sake" (1994d, 43).[16] While this emphasis on the game, on detection as sport, might seem to make light of their work, it serves another purpose. Knowing, as the reader does, that this Game is of international importance, it shows the English reader what both police and imperial reformers have tried to show for years: that authority and liberty, security and English values, can be reconciled in the figure of the detective at work.

Most important, Doyle represents Holmes's work, like that of Kim's, as the investigation of international intrigue. In addition to the aforementioned work in "The Adventure of The Bruce-Partington Plans," Holmes comes out of retirement to catch German spies in "His Last Bow" and solves crimes stemming from Mormonism in the United States (*A Study in Scarlet*) to the mutiny in India (*The Sign of the Four*). In "The Naval Treaty," when Watson is pestered by an acquaintance as to Holmes's crime-solving abilities "where such large interests are at stake," he replies, "To my certain knowledge he has acted on behalf of three of the reigning Houses of Europe in very vital matters" (1994f, 241).

The critical tradition likes to think of these stories as aberrations, with Doyle whimsically wandering into the foreign territory of Kipling, his favorite writer. And if not an aberration, then they represent Doyle's experimental effort to reduce imperial intrigue to domestic intrigue. For example, a brother's debts are at the heart of the crime in "The Adventure of The Bruce-Partington Plans" and a wife's cover-up of a youthful indiscretion begins the events in "The Second Stain." But considering Doyle's persistent imbrication of foreign and domestic worlds, it makes better sense to assume that in an age of Empire, the domestic has indeed become international and vice versa. As a result, the difference between the knowledge required of the detective, on the one hand, and of the imperial agent, on the other, becomes similarly impossible to maintain. Failure to understand the importance of cross-indexing knowledge shatters the illusion of omniscience on which the English power of surveillance depends. This is bracingly clear as Doyle's and Kipling's detectives attempt to master the heterogeneous British social world. As Holmes explains in "The Second Stain," "The man's death is a mere incident—a trivial episode—in comparison with our real task, which is to trace this document and save a European catastrophe" (1994g, 306). Indeed, a characterization of England as insular becomes the downfall of German spies in "His Last Bow." Baron Von Herling describes "Englanders" as having "their insular conventions

which simply *must* be observed" (1994d, 156). Ten pages later this famous
German agent and his colleague, Von Bork, will be outsmarted by Holmes,
who has observed *them* by infiltrating their global network as Altamont, an
American spy: "I started my pilgrimage at Chicago, graduated in an Irish
secret society at Buffalo, gave serious trouble to the constabulary at Skibbereen
and so eventually caught the eye of a subordinate agent of Von Bork" (1994d,
168).

That domestic police work is international in scope is not Doyle's point
alone. The detective can sit in the center of London and police the world.[17]
Andrew Wynter's article in *The Quarterly Review* describes Scotland Yard as
"the brain or central ganglion which directs the system of the Metropolitan
Police." This article captures the international scope of this domestic policing
as it shows Scotland Yard containing both constables who are "reading the
morning and country papers, to learn what is doing that may require their
presence" and "foreign detectives, who watch over the *mauvais sujets* from
abroad. The entire floating foreign population in the metropolis is well
known to the police" (1856, 168–69). Like Dickens's Inspector Field, who
policed the Empire while patrolling the British Museum, Holmes personifies
this system:

> he loved to lie in the very centre of five millions of people, with his filaments
> stretching out and running through them, responsive to every little rumour
> or suspicion of unsolved crime. . . . his only change was when he turned his
> mind from the evil-doer of the town to track down his brother of the coun-
> try. (1994b, 30)

But as we know from Holmes's adventures, Doyle's "town" is a clearinghouse
of *mauvais sujets* from "all parts of the habitable globe" and his "country"
extends past a distinctly foreign English countryside (*The Hound of the
Baskervilles*) to India (*The Sign of the Four*) and America (*A Study in Scarlet*).

In a famous passage, Kim, like Holmes, experiences himself at the center
of a world united by the Great Game.

> Well is the Game called great! I was four days a scullion at Quetta, waiting
> on the wife of the man whose book I stole. And that was part of the Great
> Game! From the South—God knows how far—came up the Mahratta, play-
> ing the Great Game in fear of his life. Now I shall go far and far into the
> North playing the Great Game. Truly, it runs like a shuttle throughout all
> Hind. . . . and I am Kim—Kim—Kim—alone—one person—in the middle
> of it all. (273)

In using the same description of the detective at the center of the imperial world in India, rather than in London, Kipling illustrates that the detective now embodies the center while registering both the imperial scope of English power and the indistinguishability of the center from the margin, the detective's work from that of the spy. It has been tempting for critics to see the two figures as distinct because they have separate jurisdictions: One figure has local authority and one global. But what nineteenth-century detective narratives have shown is that in an age of Empire, strict attention to jurisdictions not only interferes with crime solving but also obscures the international range—indeed potential—of English authority.[18]

Kipling's and Doyle's detectives, at the center of the imperial world "wherever [they] go," are masters of information about that world.[19] Strickland is "perpetually 'going Fantee' among natives" (Kipling 1987, 51). Kipling describes the resulting breadth of the detective's knowledge:

> He was initiated into the *Sat Bhai* at Allahabad once, when he was on leave. He knew the Lizard-Song of the Sansis, and the *Halli-Hukk* dance, which is a religious can-can of a startling kind. When a man knows who dance the *Halli-Hukk,* and how, and when, and where, he knows something to be proud of. He has gone deeper than the skin. But Strickland was not proud, though he had helped once, at Jagadhri, at the Painting of the Death Bull, which no Englishman must even look upon; had mastered the thieves'-patter of the *changars;* had taken a Yusufzai horse-thief alone near Attock; and had stood under the sounding-board of a Border mosque and conducted service in the manner of a Sunni Mullah. (52)

But as Kim learns from Lurgan Sahib, such bits of local knowledge are not for their own sake, but are part of a larger system of information, much as the pieces of a water jug that Kim breaks appear to coalesce magically before his eyes (201–2). And at the end of "Miss Youghal's *Sais,*" Kipling notes, however ruefully, that despite his going native, Strickland "fills in his Department returns beautifully" (56). It would be repetitive to illustrate all the examples of Kim's and Holmes's respective commands of local knowledge—there is not a page in which these two detectives *do not* demonstrate such knowledge. But it is significant, as further proof of the indistinguishability of domestic and international detective work, that Holmes and Creighton are so similarly characterized, as well. Holmes is constantly referencing his range of anthropological and ethnographical knowledge, whether he is citing his "two short monographs" on the human ear "in last year's *Anthropological Journal*" (1994b, 43) or using the difference between "the skull of a negro from that of an Esquimau" (1994e, 22) to demonstrate one of his central precepts: how subtle differences are obvious to the trained observer. Creighton, Kim's boss in the Great Game, is similarly a published expert in anthropology and ethnography. He demonstrates the range of his local knowledge by speaking in the vernacular, as Holmes does when playing the American agent.

Both Kipling and Doyle define detection as the integration of local knowledge.[20] So when Holmes tells Watson that they, unlike the police who investigate two crimes separately, "know of both events, and can trace the relation between them" (1994g, 300), he is not so much challenging the authority of the police as representing the ideal of a whole history of policing: from the Fieldings's police gazette to Colquhoun's plan for the centralization of information from various jurisdictions; from Sleeman's use of a network of information to bring down the Thugs to Dickens's celebration of the New Police's "incessant system of communication" to Collins's making Murthwaite's detailed imperial information central to Cuff's domestic detection.

Police history becomes imperial history—and vice versa—in the above list because the premise of Victorian policing is the premise of Victorian imperialism: Knowledge is more effective than violence in the acquisition and maintenance of authority. Of course, this is not to say that the actual history of either the police or the Empire is without significant violence. And indeed, Doyle, the author of *To Arms!*, is no foe of warfare. But violence is inferior to detective work as a way of maintaining authority, as he demonstrates when Holmes shows the mystified Watson how he read the Afghan war veteran's mind: "Your hand stole towards your own old wound and a smile quivered on your lips, which showed me that the ridiculous side of this method of settling international questions had forced itself upon your mind" (1994b, 33).

Kipling is no pacifist, either. But critics almost always comment on *Kim's* lack of violence,[21] and Kipling constantly underscores the necessity of local knowledge in running an empire, whether it is in *Kim's* argument for the Indian-born English ruler or the disasters that befall the ignorant in his Strickland stories. Creighton tells Kim that he has "known boys newly entered into the service of the Government who feigned not to understand the talk or the customs of black men. Their pay was cut for ignorance. There is no sin so great as ignorance. Remember this" (167). Kim gets a native to take him through Lahore, and he tells "Kim many astounding things where an English guide would have talked of the Mutiny" (168). Kipling emphasizes here that to see the imperial world in terms of violent occasions rather than occasions for knowledge is a crucial mistake, one a promising detective does not make.

The high price of ignorance of native life is the moral of the Strickland stories "The Return of Imray" and "The Mark of the Beast."[22] In the former,

Strickland discovers that a missing civil servant, Imray, has been killed by his native servant, who believed that Imray had put a curse on his young son (in reality he died from fever). Imray met his death "simply and solely through not knowing the nature of the Oriental and the coincidence of a little seasonal fever" (302). In "The Mark of the Beast," Strickland's drunken friend Fleete boorishly desecrates a local temple and offends a resident mystic, the "Silver Man," who then puts a curse on Fleete. Strickland is shown having contempt for Fleete's ignorance of native sensibilities and returns twice to the temple in order to apologize, but when Fleete appears to be turning into a kind of were-wolf, Strickland steps in to solve the mystery. Unlike Strickland, "who knows as much of natives of India as is good for any man" (170), the doctor he calls in to diagnose Fleete's condition fails to draw correct inferences from the evidence. "He is dead now," Kipling states succinctly (170). That both local knowledge and an ability to restore order through this knowledge rather than through violence are distinctly English principles is evident in the one time knowledge fails. Unable to reverse the hex placed on Fleete, Strickland and his Watsonian sidekick have to beat cooperation out of the Silver Man. Kipling, who does not describe the torture—"this part is not to be printed" (183)—simply writes that "we had fought for Fleete's soul with the Silver Man in that room and had disgraced ourselves as Englishmen forever" (190).

It is tempting to see this emphasis on the power of knowledge, as not a few critics have, as evidence of a sure-footed imperial panopticism at work in both Kipling and Doyle. While I do not want to suggest that either Kipling or Doyle are opposed to authority at home or abroad, I think an emphasis on them as the bards of a confident and effortless jingoism has overlooked the dialogue about what both comprises and compromises imperial authority— and English identity itself—at the heart of their fiction and the detective genre as a whole. While their detective figures certainly "have the state at [their] back[s]" (1994a, 56), they are, like their detective predecessors, critics of the state, as well. It is a leitmotif of Holmes criticism to point out the places where he shows up officialdom, whether in the form of the public police or in dastardly noblemen. Doyle writes in "The Naval Treaty" of "that not too common type, a nobleman who is in truth noble" (1994f, 233). Holmes often makes the point to Watson that the law is often as much an obstacle to truth as crime: "It is a case, my dear Watson, where the law is as dangerous to us as the criminals are" (1994g, 306). Strickland's excellence has, we recall, "done him no good in the Indian Government" (1987, 51). And for every "friend of all the world" like Kim, Kipling has a rebarbative Fleete. A contempt, albeit lighthearted, for the official police runs through *Kim,* as well: "What fools are these Police Sahibs," Kim exclaims "genially" (256).

The criticism of official authority here and throughout the tradition of detective and imperial narratives is not a renunciation of authority, but an argument for the necessity of better authority through a centralized system of local knowledge. The systematization of knowledge requires constant forays into the domain of the local and peripheral, not an insulated surveillance from the center. Far from pushing that which is un-English to the margins, Kipling and Doyle show that being an *English* detective means needing to know native life from the uncanny alleys of London to the grim moors of Devonshire, from the backstreets of Lahore to the Grand Trunk Road. The effect of this emphasis on expanding the range of local knowledge is to make the colonial world, the "outré," part of what it means to be English.

This reading of Kipling's and Doyle's representation of a center defined by constant traffic with the peripheral explains an aspect of their fiction for which the critical tradition has failed to provide a satisfactory explanation: the presence of the supernatural. So far as magic illustrates the limits of rational knowledge, its presence would necessarily pose a problem for narratives that sought only to insist on the power of modern knowledge. Brantlinger's category of the "imperial Gothic" importantly shows a connection between imperialism and the fin-de-siècle interest in magic. But in a perfect example of the will to separate domestic from exotic narratives, Brantlinger overlooks Doyle's detective fiction and includes only his *The Lost World* and "supernatural" stories among his examples of the imperial gothic.

In these stories, he contends, the occult returns home from the colonial periphery to the metropolitan center. In assuming that Doyle's detection stories obey the literary critical distinction between domestic and foreign, Brantlinger consequently joins those readers who consider Doyle's turn to spiritualism an embarrassing or at least irreconcilable move for the Poet Laureate of English empiricism, as uncharacteristic of Sir Arthur as it is of Sherlock Holmes to enter into espionage.[23] The critical tradition's abiding predisposition to consign Holmes to a rigid category of rational modernity allows us to forget that the appearance of the occult, as the "hell-hound" of the Devonshire moors, shapes Doyle's most acclaimed Holmes novel, *The Hound of the Baskervilles*. Dr. Mortimer, "a trained man of science," brings the case to Holmes and suggests that he thinks there might be something to a supernatural explanation of events. He says this in private because "a man of science shrinks from placing himself in the public position of seeming to indorse a popular superstition" (11). In solving the mystery, let us not forget, Holmes refuses to discredit the supernatural:

> Of course, if Dr. Mortimer's surmise should be correct, and we are dealing
> with forces outside the ordinary laws of Nature, there is an end of our inves-

tigation. But we are bound to exhaust all other hypotheses before falling back
upon this one. (19)

On this note, he leaves the interpenetration of modern core and primitive
periphery perfectly intact, suggesting that the distinction is little more than a
comforting fiction. To no one's surprise, the presence of the supernatural per-
vades Kipling's imperial adventure stories. It should nevertheless surprise us
to find that "forces outside the ordinary laws of Nature" are no less present in
his detective stories. While Strickland saves his friend Fleete from turning
into a werewolf, he can no more rationalize the supernatural mysteries of the
curse than do the vampire hunters in Bram Stoker's novel. Strickland simply
has to force the Silver Man to undo the curse.

In showing the detective taking seriously that which is beyond the bounds
of his own vast expertise, Kipling and Doyle rather illustrate that the English
detective's beat is not limited to the limiting timetables and charts of Sayers's
"knowable universe."[24] Strickland's sidekick, attempting to provide closure to
the supernatural mystery in "The Mark of the Beast," begins to quote
Hamlet: "There are more things. . . ."[25] Strickland, the consummate detective, cuts him off: "Strickland hates that quotation. He says that I have worn
it threadbare" (190). While Strickland attempts to know everything, he cannot. "Strickland hates being mystified by natives," Kipling writes, "because
his business in life is to overmatch them with their own weapons. He has not
yet succeeded in doing this, but in 15 or 20 years he will have made some
small progress" (175).

In a passage in the middle of *Kim,* the detective master Lurgan Sahib
explains to Kim those men who excel at the Game:

> From time to time, God causes men to be born—and thou are one of them—
> who have a lust to go abroad at the risk of their lives and discover news—
> today it may be of far-off things, tomorrow of some hidden mountain, and
> the next day of some near-by men who have done a foolishness against the
> State. (209)

Here in the middle of "the greatest of all spy novels," Kipling sums up the
achievement of one hundred years of detective fiction. In this one sentence,
he links the detective and the explorer, the discovery of information and State
security, and the connection between knowledge of "far-off things" and those
"near-by." Most important, he emphasizes to a receptive audience (in both
Kim and the English reader) that these men are heroes. It took a long time
for detective narratives to reimagine the un-English paramilitary figure of the

late-eighteenth century as the heroic imperial detective represented here. But in reimagining this figure over the course of a long nineteenth century, writers from Godwin and Mill to Kipling and Doyle did no less than reimagine English identity in an age of Empire.

⇥5⇤

CONCLUSION

When Edmund Burke, during the trial of Warren Hastings, exclaims, "God forbid it should be said that no nation under heaven equals the British in substantial violence and in formal justice" (Bond 1:10), he fires the opening salvo in the nineteenth-century struggle to reimagine British authority as essentially nonviolent. The project of reimagining authority as nonviolent through the idea of detection is shared by the diverse works discussed in this book: from Godwin's and James Mill's criticisms of imperial authority to the problems faced by anxious colonial administrators in solving the mysteries of Thuggee; from the nonthreatening methods of Dickens's Bucket or Collins's Cuff to Doyle's and Kipling's representations of Empire as intelligence work. The figure of the detective is one of the chief vehicles for this reimagination: The story of replacing violent with nonviolent power is his story, too. From turn-of-the-century associations of detection with spying to Peterloo-era fears of a paramilitary police, the figure of the detective had a long way to go before he could sit snugly in his armchair at Baker Street. This is not to say that the detective represents a check on the idea of British power. When W. O'Brien writes in the *Edinburgh Review* that the "soldier is necessarily a bad policeman" (1852, 10–11), he is not limiting the authority of the police (before whom, we recall from chapter 3, the mob would still quail), but rather reimagining it.

The Victorian era was a time of the consolidation of almost bewildering authority in terms of both domestic institutions and global influence. The field of Victorian Studies, if one can refer to such a diverse range of scholarship as a single field, has persuasively mapped out the operations of this power, from works inspired by Edward Said's seminal *Orientalism* (1978) to D. A. Miller's extraordinarily influential work on the Victorian novel, *The Novel and the Police* (1988). In the wake of persuasive applications of Foucault's paradigm of power/knowledge and specifically his theory of "panopticism," and Miller's as well, it has been easy to read nineteenth-century fiction as being at the center of, to use Miller's term, a "carceral" society. The idea of panopticism has been particularly dominant in two areas of literary criticism: (1) readings of detective fiction and (2) readings of imperial literature. Indeed the Victorian detective, with gimlet gaze and myriad disguises, or his counterpart, the Victorian colonial administrator armed with maps and glossaries, would seem perfectly to demonstrate the rise of a kind of panoptical power in a carceral culture, whether at home or abroad. As I have been arguing throughout this book, however, we need to have a more nuanced understanding of the profound and confusing struggles that went along with conceiving and implementing such authority. If the marriage of benevolence and power embodied by Sherlock Holmes was as natural as the critical tradition would have us believe, the Great Detective would have been invented at the beginning of the nineteenth century and thus covered at the beginning, rather than at the ending, of a work on fictions of detection.

While we have read detective fiction and imperial literature similarly, we have read them separately.[1] This has been my other aim in this book: to argue that nineteenth-century literature reveals how the administration of the British Empire and the development of the domestic detective depended on one another. I have wanted this work to be part of what David Cannadine describes as putting "the history of Britain back into the history of empire, and the history of the empire back into the history of Britain" (xx). We need to examine these now-familiar figures of the detective and the imperial explorer *together* in their proper global context, the "vast, interconnected world" in which the detective is brought to life amidst anxieties about increasing imperial power and the imperial explorer is shaped by domestic ideas about power.[2] It is particularly important because, as we have seen, these two figures at times seem to tell the opposite story of a world more aptly characterized as "us versus them." But what these two figures together reveal is how the acquisition of local knowledge, whether gathered in the back alleys of London or Lahore, destabilizes the rigid understanding of place that the panopticon turned into architecture. The detective figure shows us how constant forays into the peripheries define and continually redefine the center, giving the Victorian nation that the detective comes to represent a more contingent identity than we have heretofore allowed. By situating the figure of the detective in this vast, interconnected world, rather than as the home-grown gatekeeper of a narrowly envisioned metropolitan center, we restore to detective fiction the critique of authority out of which it first came. It was a critique, we have seen, from all sides of the political spectrum: from radical Godwin to Utilitarian Mill to complex conservatives in Doyle and Kipling.

Reading the history of detective fiction as a history of skepticism about authority questions one of the most pervasive critical assumptions about the genre: that, to paraphrase Miller, detective fiction performs a simplification of power, or, to quote Franco Moretti, that detective fiction is "liberalism's executioner" (155).[3]

The lesson of *Detecting the Nation* is that the demands of an imperial world called the English detective reluctantly into being but that in detecting that imperial nation he made the Empire part of what it meant to be English in the Victorian period. This is also the lesson of John Buchan's *The Thirty-Nine Steps*, a reading of which will conclude this book. *The Thirty-Nine Steps* can be read as a minihistory of the detective, from his origins as a criminal, vaguely foreign outsider to his ultimate place as embodiment of English law and order. Buchan's novel, however, has traditionally been read not as a detective story but rather as one of the first spy thrillers. Appearing in 1915, around the same time as many of the generically challenged Holmes stories discussed in the previous chapter, *The Thirty-Nine Steps* is an example par excellence of both the critical tendency to see stories about imperial intrigue as altogether different from stories of domestic detection, as well as my point that these two genres are in fact the same story about what authority can and should look like in an age of Empire. *The Thirty-Nine Steps* tells the story of how an imperial outsider, Richard Hannay, a restless young mining engineer recently returned to England from South Africa, becomes an Englishman and learns to detect impostors in a world in which national identity appears to be a masquerade. As detective fiction demonstrated throughout the long nineteenth century, distinguishing between the center and the margin is almost impossible, a point underscored in a conversation between Hannay and a fellow countryman: "D'you think that adventure is found only in the tropics . . . Maybe you're rubbing shoulders with it at this moment." "That's what Kipling says," his companion agrees (22). That Kipling would be an expert on adventures in the British countryside is the very situation that gives rise to the English detective and now to Richard Hannay.

RICHARD HANNAY DETECTS THE NATION

In his introduction to *The Thirty-Nine Steps*, Alan Weissman suggests that "the author found the exact recipe for an emerging genre and with it created a perfect instance of the type" (iii), a type called by many titles, from espionage and suspense to, in Buchan's own words, a "shocker" (v). Early in Buchan's novel, an innkeeper who hears Hannay's story of international intrigue draws "his

breath in sharply" and whispers "By God! . . . it is all pure Rider Haggard and
Conan Doyle" (22). The "literary innkeeper," as Buchan calls him, knows
what literary tradition has forgotten: The imperial adventure stories of
Haggard and domestic detective stories of Conan Doyle are not different types
of stories but rather part of a seamless story about British power in the world.
But much like the partition of Kipling from Doyle, Buchan's novel is taken to
illustrate the opposite: a seam. In a fascinating reading of the first Sherlock
Holmes novella, *A Study in Scarlet*, Joseph McLaughlin talks about the difficulty critics have had reading the significant portion of the novel that takes
place in a Mormon community in nineteenth-century America. McLaughlin
argues that "we need to read the novel's mixed generic quality as a clue to the
novelist's desire to tell a story for which there does not yet exist a seamless form"
(38). I heartily share with McLaughlin the position that placing strict generic
boundaries around the work of Doyle causes us to overlook the important cultural work the Holmes stories do. I would argue, however, that there already
existed a seamless form: The nineteenth-century detective narrative has no
borders. It is in the critical compartmentalization of Doyle, as well as writers
like Buchan who are similarly read as inaugurating genres, that we are watching the seam being sewn. Writers like Kipling and Buchan are placed on the
other side of that seam, which makes Buchan part of a different tradition, even
though, as Weissman later writes in the introduction, "*The Thirty-Nine Steps*
also owes much to the crime fiction of the second half of the nineteenth century, particularly that of Arthur Conan Doyle" (iii). My work in this book has
been to show why the tradition of detective fiction should not be separated
from the adventure/spy tradition and what we overlook when we do so. In my
introduction I suggest that *Detecting the Nation* is an attempt to address three
questions I felt were not adequately explained in existing accounts of detective
fiction: (1) how the threateningly foreign police become English; (2) how
accepting the police facilitates an acceptance of imperial authority; and (3)
how the margin comes to define the center. *The Thirty-Nine Steps* will help me
to address these questions one last time.

Certainly, there is much superficial evidence in Buchan's novel to prove his
debt to Doyle and the continuity of his work with Victorian fictions of detection. Buchan's chapter titles sound like the titles of Holmes stories, such as
"The Adventure of the Radical Candidate" and "The Adventure of the Bald
Archaeologist." Like Holmes, Hannay spends some smoke-filled sleepless
nights puzzling out the case (25) and even draws the comparison indirectly:
"I wasn't any kind of Sherlock Holmes. But I have always fancied I had a kind
of instinct about questions like this" (74). Hannay, like our earlier detective
figures, Caleb Williams and Gabriel Betteredge, comes down with a strong

case of "detective fever" in which "an abominable restlessness had taken possession of me" (67). While Hannay seems at home in the family of English detectives, what is even more important is the point that Buchan is careful to make: Hannay is *not* a spy. While many critics see *The Thirty-Nine Steps* as a defining moment in the emergence of the spy novel, Hannay is much more accurately understood as a detective. Buchan, nodding to the detective's early struggles to disassociate himself from the French figure of the spy, has Royer, a Frenchman, describe "the habits of the spy." Saying that "we in France know something of the breed," Royer describes the spy as someone who "receives personally his reward, and he delivers personally his intelligence" (73). Hannay's interest is never strictly personal; his self-centered, Holmes-like ennui quickly wears off as Scudder, the man whom he had been harboring, is murdered. As Hannay decodes the international mysteries in Scudder's little black book and runs from the murderers, his motive becomes far more about the security of his country than of himself.

But even as Hannay strives to save England, he does not initially identify with England. As he questions his own Englishness, he questions the very presumption of any kind of natural English identity in a time when, in the heart of London, "a lot of Imperialist ladies asked me to tea to meet schoolmasters from New Zealand and editors from Vancouver" (1). "The talk of the ordinary Englishman made me sick," explains Hannay, who "had been three months in the Old Country, and was fed up with it" (1). Having made his "pile" in South Africa, Hannay is back in England. But "my father had brought me out from Scotland at the age of six, and I had never been home since; so England was a sort of Arabian Nights to me" (1). Fictions of detection have been at pains to make the detective English: Godwin's attempt to show a natural English instinct for truth and curiosity in Caleb's "unadorned tale" becomes Dickens's representation of the homegrown virtues of his detective police; Collins uses the old English rose as the symbol of his detective, Cuff; Holmes famously retires from his bohemian Baker Street to a life of beekeeping in the English countryside. The task of *The Thirty-Nine Steps,* like the process dramatized in detective fiction over the long nineteenth century, is to make an Englishman out of the alienated Hannay. As the novel goes on, Hannay finds himself back in England and begins to relax:

> After Scotland the air smelt heavy and flat, but infinitely sweet, for the limes and chestnuts and lilac bushes were domes of blossom. . . . Somehow the place soothed me and put me at my ease. I fell to whistling as I looked into the green depths, and the tune which came to my lips was "Annie Laurie" . (58–59)

Hannay is literally saved by his native landscape when his car smashes into the bed of a stream, "but a branch of hawthorn got me in the chest, lifted me up and held me, while a ton or two of expensive metal slipped below me" (29).

While finding the British countryside comforting is something Hannay shares with nineteenth-century detectives, finding it full of a confusing imperial presence is something *The Thirty-Nine Steps* shares with Victorian detective fiction. As Dickens's detective anecdotes and Collins's *The Moonstone* turned England into the Empire before the eyes of the necessary detective, Hannay, too, constantly sees the imperial periphery at home. A little railroad station in Scotland "reminded me of one of those forgotten little stations in the Karroo" (17); elsewhere Sir Harray tells Hannay that "you can put a week among the shepherds, and be as safe as if you were in New Guinea" (34). What the detective has taught us through his own transformation is that national identity is not an essential quality, but something more like a masquerade; it is at once recognizable and unstable.[4] Which is why it is something the detective can wear, as Hannay does here: "when I left that cottage I was the living image of the kind of Scotsman you see in the illustrations to Burns's poems" (56).

In Hannay, then, we have a character who underscores the precarious struggle involved in the production of national identity. Being English does not come naturally to this child of the veld, but he understands how to wear it as a disguise. Rather than suggesting a cynical understanding of national identity, however, Buchan here shows that through being a detective literally on the margins of English society, Hannay comes to understand what it really means to be English. His representation of Hannay as a detective draws from those of the writers discussed in this work. First, he is recognizable to and respectful of the average Briton. Even though Hannay is wanted as the Portland Place murderer, many locals overlook this as they choose to trust him instead. Like Gabriel Betteredge who says, "I couldn't help liking the Sergeant—though I hated him all the time" (Wilkie Collins 200), a bystander helps out Hannay after a car crash explaining only moments after meeting him, "You're the right sort of fellow" (29). Hannay later reflects, "Obviously Sir Walter believed in me, though why he did I could not guess" (60). Hannay returns the favor and sounds the same trusting, reassuring tone as Bucket and Cuff before him: "Listen Sir Harry, I've got something pretty important to say to you. You're a good fellow and I'm going to be frank" (32). Hannay relies on locals because he understands what Mill's ideal legislator, Colonel Sleeman, Inspector Bucket, Sergeant Cuff, Holmes, Strickland, and Creighton understood before him: the importance of local knowledge. Being almost a stranger to his "home," he understands that "my lack of local knowledge might very well be

my undoing" (45). He understands that the detective does not have panoptical vision; to do his work he must trust in multiple sources of local knowledge,
such as in the conclusion when Hannay gets a crucial piece of information
about the "thirty-nine steps" from a local coastguard man. His own colonial
knowledge is just another form of that local knowledge and his expertise here,
like that of *The Moonstone*'s Murthwaite, comes in just as handy in the metropolitan center. Not only does his colonial experience (from knife tricks to
hunting stories) allow him to engage and impress his many helpers, but the
skills honed on the imperial periphery enable Hannay to survive and save the
English nation: "Now my life on the veld has given me the eyes of a kite, and
I can see things for which most men need a telescope" (36).

While Hannay might have unusual abilities, Buchan insists on an almost
nostalgic nonviolence in his representation of the detective. Hannay is no
James Bond, master of technology and weaponry, a point made obvious in
having him pursued by cutting-edge technology circa 1915—an aeroplane—
while he has only his legs and, for a brief time, a bicycle to elude capture. No
one is hurt when Hannay blows up the residence of the "Bald Archaeologist"
who is holding him captive. Recalling the lesson that a soldier is necessarily a
bad policeman, Hannay comments at the end, as he is about to go join the
fight in World War I, that "I had done my best service . . . *before I put on
khaki*" (88, my emphasis).

Through local knowledge, nonviolence, and a respect bordering on love for
the inhabitants and landscape of his native Britain, we see how the foreign
figure of Hannay becomes not only part of his country, but its only hope. As
The Thirty-Nine Steps shows the figure of the detective to be a product of both
the imperial periphery and the metropolitan center, it also shows a successful
marriage of both skepticism about and faith in authority. Initially, Hannay,
like the reader, wonders whom he can trust and the question of the character
of British authority is put into play. "My first impulse had been to write a letter to the Prime Minister, but a little reflection convinced me that that would
be useless" (28). Crucially, Hannay is equally on the run from the British
police, who want him for the murder, *and* from the Black Stone, the enemies
of the British state. As the novel goes on, and as Hannay begins to embody
more and more of the characteristics of the traditional detective, he begins to
"think wistfully of the police . . . They at any rate were fellow-countrymen
and honest men, and their tender mercies would be kinder than these ghoul-
ish aliens" (49–50). By the final chapters of the novel, Hannay is literally
teamed with Scotland Yard (74), and when asked by the three members of
the Black Stone, who are impersonating proper Englishmen, "Where do you
come from?" he answers, "Scotland Yard" (83–84).

The story of the detective in the nineteenth century has shown us how the margins come to define the center. *The Thirty-Nine Steps* shows us this literally in having a mining engineer gradually work his way from South Africa to Scotland to England to prospect for truth at the heart of the nation. But *The Thirty-Nine Steps* demonstrates the more serious theoretical implications of this trajectory as well. Buchan's novel is no less than a theory of national identity in a world defined by masquerade. If the concept of panopticism suggests that power can be characterized by the figure of the guard who safely scans the periphery from an invisible point in the center, *The Thirty-Nine Steps* turns this formulation on its head. Since its origins at the end of the eighteenth century, detective fiction has examined new ways of seeing in a world in which the relationship between seeing and knowing is radically destabilized. In *Caleb Williams,* Falkland appears to be the very model of a kindhearted master, but Caleb learns otherwise and must flee, Hannay-like, through the wilds of his native land, in order to get at the plain truth. Colonel Sleeman and Captain Taylor are at once flummoxed and entranced by the deception of the Thugs. While Bucket has near-omniscient powers of seeing, the world of *Bleak House* is one in which a lifelong London resident, Snagsby, can scarcely believe what he is seeing when he accompanies the detective to Tom-all-alone's and Lady Dedlock, disguised as a streetwoman, manages to elude Bucket. *The Moonstone* stages this very problem between seeing and knowing in its reenactment of the drug-induced theft of the diamond, and Watson continually inhabits the same problem as he meets an opium addict or a drunken groom only to find that he is in fact Holmes in disguise. The ne plus ultra of the difficult relationship between knowing and seeing is the famous passage near the end of *Kim:*

> He tried to think of the lama . . . but the bigness of the world . . . swept linked thought aside. Then he looked upon the trees and the broad fields . . . looked with strange eyes unable to take up the size and proportion, and use of things—stared for a still half-hour. All that while he felt, though he could not put it into words, that his soul was out of gear with its surroundings. (331)

The fantasy of both Empire and the police is that the colonizer or detective can see with "imperial eyes" and that seeing is tantamount to knowing and mastering. Indeed, after Kim's momentary lapse, Kipling demonstrates this fantasy as Kim "felt the wheels of his being lock up anew on the world without. Things that rode meaningless on the eyeball an instant before slid into proper proportion" (331). Despite the fantasy of *Kim*, fictions of detection more often than not expose this as a fantasy as the detective's world is the murky reality of red herrings, disguise, counterfeiting and forgeries, mistaken identities and impersonations. Detectives, then, are not people who have panoptical vision—as we have seen, the vision of detectives is in fact as qualified in detective stories as it is celebrated—but who understand the precarious, even treacherous nature of what you see and how that, as in the example from *Kim,* relates to a precarious state of being.

As *The Thirty-Nine Steps* draws to a close and Hannay has tracked the three German members of the Black Stone to a tennis court on the English coast, he is puzzled by what appear to be "three ordinary, game-playing, suburban Englishmen" (80). Suddenly Hannay remembers the theory of old Peter Pienaar, "the best scout I ever knew," who, like the nineteenth-century detective, was "pretty often on the windy side of the law . . . before he had turned respectable" (81). Hannay describes Peter's theory that

> if a man could get into perfectly different surroundings from those in which he had been first observed, and—this is the important part—really play up to these surroundings and behave as if he had never been out of them, he would puzzle the cleverest detectives on earth. (81)

Or *be* the cleverest detective on earth. For *The Thirty-Nine Steps* shows us how detective work is a metaphor for identity. Another "maxim of Peter's," Hannay discloses, is "if you are playing a part, you will never keep it up unless you convince yourself that you are *it*" (81). The detective, through his own transformation from outsider to insider over the nineteenth century, shows us how national identity is at once a part you play and a thing you become. The precarious nature of national identity is why the detective, someone who can detect impostors and police these constantly shifting borders, is necessary. If we allow ourselves to see the detective as a homegrown emanation of the metropolitan center, completely distinct from such other figures as the colonial explorer (or mining engineer), we overlook this important lesson about identity in the Victorian period. Hannay knows better, rubs his eyes, and takes another look. Putting detective fiction back into the vast, interconnected world that produced it asks us to do the same.

NOTES

NOTES TO INTRODUCTION

1. Doyle's lamentation is reflected in the apologetic tone—and its flip side, the defensiveness—of many critical treatments of detective fiction, which seem always to be responding to Edmund Wilson's (in)famous essay "Who Cares Who Killed Roger Ackroyd?" Winks's introduction to *Detective Fiction*, for example, is a defense of the genre's overlooked literariness. See also Most and Stowe, and Walker and Frazer, whose collections look at detective fiction through a range of contemporary literary theories, none of which, curiously enough, allows the reader to move beyond the formal limits traditionally placed on the genre.

2. In saying that most accounts of the genre overlook the role of detective fiction in the construction of an imperialist national identity, I do not want to imply that these diverse accounts have the same understanding of literature's relationship (or lack thereof) to history. For example, the only thing that Julian Symons's breezy if insightful *Bloody Murder* has in common with D. A. Miller's theoretically rigorous *The Novel and the Police* is that neither thinks the genre has anything to do with the rise of the British Empire. Treatments of detective fiction, such as works by Symons, Knight, Porter, Winks, the authors collected in Most and Stowe, Walker and Frazer, and Thomas A. Seebok and Umberto Eco, as well as essays by Moretti, Slavos Zizek, and Miller, encompass a range of critical perspectives from formalism and semiotics to Marxism and deconstruction. But in establishing the genre's significant and unique qualities, these diverse works collaboratively establish it as a distinct genre, which separates it from other contemporaneous types of writing. Treating the rise of detective fiction and the rise of Empire as parts of the same cultural project makes it harder to accept Miller's influential suggestion that detective fiction performs "a drastic simplification of power" (69). On the contrary, I contend, detective fiction performs the cultural work of connecting complex cultural debates operating in many different discursive sites.

3. The following brief history of the detective is a condensed version of an entry I wrote for *The Encyclopedia of the Victorian Era*. When the Metropolitan Police Act was passed in 1829, England was one of the last European countries to have an organized police force. The idea of an organized police grew in response to early-nineteenth-century concerns about increasing crime as well as to widespread objections to an arbitrary and overly harsh legal system. Additionally, there was growing concern that law enforcement was a privilege of the wealthy as private police had to be hired for the detection and solution of crime. As Sir Robert Peel, who inherited reform from Sir Samuel Romilly and Sir James Mackintosh, put it "the country has outgrown her police institutions." As Home Secretary for most of the 1820s, Peel established the Metropolitan

Police in 1829 as a distinctly unmilitary force, unarmed and uniformed in top hats and blue tailed-coats. Professionalism and prevention of crime, rather than detection and the solution of crimes, were the cornerstone of Peel's police, called "peelers" and later "bobbies." But public fears of a standing army and of a violation of personal liberties insured that the evolution of the police and of the detective in particular would be gradual. Reservations about the detective still lingered from the eighteenth century, when, according to Ian Ousby, "the thief-taker could seem as disturbing a figure as the criminal himself" (*Bloodhounds*). Until 1842, when a small detective force grew out of London's Metropolitan Police, detection of crime in England remained in the hands of private individuals or the plainclothes constables of the old police offices. Even the first police commissioners resisted the idea of detective police. Edwin Chadwick writes in the 1840s that Commissioners Rowan and Mayne "disliked detection on principle, and only yielded to its adoption on what they deemed superior authority" (qtd. in Smith 65). The Bow Street Runners, a small detective force organized in the eighteenth century by magistrates Henry and John Fielding, were the most famous predecessor to the official detective, and indeed some Runners joined the ranks of the new Metropolitan Police.

4. From the crimes covered at the Hastings Trial to Seringapatam (the historical event that begins *The Moonstone*), reformers and the public felt that England was at risk for becoming known for arbitrary violence in its colonial affairs.

5. One such reformer, Patrick Colquhoun, a noted authority on both the British Empire and metropolitan crime, explained that "London is not only the grand Magazine of the British Empire, but also the general receptacle for the idle and depraved . . . from every quarter of the dominions of the Crown" (1797, xi).

6. Burke's fiery perorations on the "high crimes" of Warren Hastings in India were an attempt to distinguish between English justice and oriental despotism—in other words, to stabilize the opposition between that which is English and that which is not English. In the second year of the trial, Burke pauses at characteristic length to clarify the stakes of this proceeding:

> This prosecution . . . is not only for the punishing a delinquent and preventing this and that offence, but a great censorial prosecution, for the purpose of preserving the manners, characters and virtues, that characterise the people of England. . . . if you teach the people of England, by the successes of those who practice this fraud, a concealing, narrow, suspicious, guarded conduct—if you teach them qualities directly contrary to those which they have hitherto been distinguished—if you make them a nation of concealers, a nation of dissemblers, a nation of liars, a nation of forgers—my Lordships, if you in one word turn them into a people of banyas—the character of England . . . will be gone and lost. . . . Today the Commons of Great Britain prosecute the delinquents of India; tomorrow the delinquents of India may be the Commons of Great Britain. (Bond 2:208–9)

Burke estimates the cost of an acquittal at literally the cost of the country; for justice to be denied here would convert a nation characterized by the absence of criminality into a nation of criminals, Indians, and Indian criminals (banyas). Employing the same language of necessity and preservation that will be used by propolice reformers, Burke claims that the nation may lose the ability to distinguish between its own government and foreign criminals, to distinguish, in "one word," between Empire and crime.

7. See E. P. Thompson. In his discussion of Peterloo (1966, see especially chap. 5), he describes how violence became an embarrassment to government.

8. Even with the use of force, colonies were being lost. Macaulay characterized the crossroads faced by a down but not out British Empire in an article on Warren Hastings. "In every part of the world," he writes,

> [England] had been a loser. Not only had she been compelled to acknowledge the independence of thirteen colonies peopled by her children, and to conciliate the Irish by giving up the right of legislating for them; but, in the Mediterranean, in the Gulf of Mexico, on the coast of Africa, on the continent of America, she had been compelled to cede the fruits of her victories in former wars. (essay on Warren Hastings 1928, 128)

9. Prevention as a reformist principle had a wider application in nineteenth-century society. As Philip Thurmond Smith notes, "the preventive idea applied to the police was not exclusive to that body. Prevention was a principle dear to the hearts of men like Bentham and his followers, notably Edwin Chadwick" (24).

10. Benedict Anderson famously suggested how nations were formed around increasingly coherent print cultures but has left it to others to suggest how national cultures are constructed largely in relation to other cultures. As Linda Colley explains, a sense of British identity is forged "not so much [from] consensus or homogeneity or centralisation at home, as a strong sense of dissimilarity from those without" (17). See also Mary Louise Pratt and Simon Gikandi. The essays in Homi K. Bhabha's collection *Nation and Narration* raise important questions about nations and storytelling. See also V. Y. Mudimbe for a consideration of how nations mutually "invent" one another. For more recent works exploring questions of Victorian national identity, see Ian Baucom, Lauren Goodlad, Katie Trumpener, and Cannon Schmitt. Work on colonial policing in the last decade has similarly emphasized how nations in a colonial relationship are mutually defined through such institutions as the police. See Mike Brogden, as well as the collection of essays *Policing the Empire* edited by David M. Anderson and David Killingray.

11. In the Oath for Initiation, members of the Detection Club of London, organized by Dorothy Sayers and Knox in the 1930s, pledged to observe "a seemly moderation in the use of Gangs, conspiracies, Death Rays, Ghosts, Hypnotism, trapdoors, Chinamen." One of Knox's commandments is that "No Chinaman must figure in the story." A fascinating recent article by Franco Moretti, "The Slaughterhouse of Literature," illustrates the ease with which literary critics still conceive of the detective story as "a very simple genre"; in Moretti's examination, the detective story can be reduced to the "formal device" of "clues."

12. This definition comes from *The Cambridge Guide to Literature in English* 271). While there are obviously many other, more developed characterizations of the formal components of the genre, my use of the *Cambridge Guide*'s definition here is purposely to provide the most basic characterization of detective fiction.

13. As Cannon Schmitt says in relation to a contemporary of the emergent detective story, the Gothic, "sheer diversity threatens categorical coherence" (5). Schmitt continues, "the Gothic, because of its particular generic incoherence, lays bare the

stakes involved in naming any genre" (6). Indeed, virtually all the major Victorian nov-els—arguably narrative itself—share with the detective story the idea that identity is produced through the solution of some mystery: Most of Dickens's novels fit this description; Jane Eyre consolidates her sense of self by solving the mystery of Rochester's relationship to the madwoman in the attic; and Dorothea Brooke reassess-es her life after the exposure of Bulstrode's mysterious past. But to consider everything a detective story is to lose any sense of what is distinct or unique about the detective genre. "Without something like a notion of genre," Schmitt writes of the Gothic, "each text can only be read as if it were *sui generis*" (6).

14. Something of the nature of this dynamic is suggested in Frantz Fanon's dis-cussion of the relativity of identity in a colonial context. See *Black Skin, White Masks,* particularly chapter 5.

15. Barbara Johnson explains in her introduction to *A World of Difference* that this book is an attempt to carry the deconstructive analyses of her earlier book *The Critical Difference* into "the real world" (2). My references to Johnson are based on these later essays.

16. While I mention Mudimbe here, see of course Said's *Orientalism* and *Culture and Imperialism.*

17. My ideas here on the chiasmatic logic of identity formation resonate with Cannon Schmitt's characterization of Zizek's "internal limit." See *Alien Nation,* 164–66.

18. The full quotation, "The thing is not—never was English," comes from the organ of Sir Robert Peel's own Tory party, *The Standard* (Reith 53).

19. See Ian Ousby's *Bloodhounds of Heaven* for a standard treatment of the genre that follows traditional police history. Hayden White challenges such narrative clas-sification, whether it be literary or historical. See in particular "The Historical Text as Literary Artifact" in *Tropics of Discourse,* and *The Content of the Form: Narrative Discourse and Historical Representation.*

20. Clive Emsley explains that

> until the 1970s police history was largely informed by a Whig view which saw
> history in relatively simple terms of progress and presupposed the emergence of
> a broad consensus in politics and society from the Victorian period. . . . They
> accepted the arguments of the police reformers of the nineteenth century. (4)

A quotation from the preface of Sir Leon Radzinowicz's classic work on English crim-inal law shows how the tradition of police history has explicitly seen itself in the Whig tradition: "Lord Macaulay's generalisation that the history of England is the history of progress is as true of the criminal law of this country as of the other social institutions of which it is a part" (1:ix). Charles Reith's hagiographic police histories provide an extreme version of this Whiggish tradition of taking as fact the steady and peaceful pro-gression of police success at home, and then naturally outward to the British borders and colonies. "In the course of thirty years," Reith explains proudly, "a 'London-model' Police Force was established in every town and country in Great Britain, and in almost every colony and dependency of the empire" (26). While tracing the evolu-tion of the police differently, most of these accounts characterize the Metropolitan Police as a nonmilitaristic embodiment of orderly English values and ignore what some recent scholars, such as Brogden, have argued convincingly: that not only is the relationship between policing the metropolitan core and the colonial periphery much more circuitous than these traditional histories suppose, but that the Metropolitan Police is in many ways an imperial creation. See also Anderson and Killingray, as well as Anand Yang, for work on the imperial context of British policing.

21. Erin O'Connor has recently suggested an interesting and, she believes, problematic relationship between Victorian Studies and Postcolonial Studies. In short, she explores the impact of Gayatri Spivak's famous essay "Three Women's Texts and a Critique of Imperialism" on Victorian Studies, suggesting that the Victorian novel has become "the genre [postcolonial theory] loves to hate" (219). My emphasis here is different; postcolonial theory is obviously important to my attempts to "world," to borrow the loaded term from both Spivak's and O'Connor's essays, the genre of detective fiction. Nevertheless, I, too, am concerned with the blind spots of theoretical paradigms, specifically Foucault's theory of panopticism.

22. It is interesting to note that Miller's reading of the nineteenth-century novel similarly moves freely between English and French works, as he explains: "Practically, the 'nineteenth-century novel' here will mean these names: Dickens, Collins, Trollope, Eliot, Balzac, Stendhal, Zola" (2).

23. As Miller himself explains in the foreword to *The Novel and the Police*, "the most notable reticence in Foucault's work concerns precisely the reading of literary texts and literary institutions, which, though often and suggestively cited in passing, are never given a role to play within the disciplinary processes under consideration" (viii).

24. "Comprehensive knowledge," Richards writes, "was the sense that knowledge was singular and not plural, complete and not partial, global and not local, that all knowledges would ultimately turn out to be concordant in one great system of knowledge" (7). Here I want to make the point that Goodlad made: There are different Foucaults. Foucault's representation of knowledge is much less totalizing, for example, in "Two Lectures" in *Power/Knowledge*. But it is the Foucault of *Discipline and Punish* that has had such a powerful effect on contemporary understanding of the figure of the detective in the nineteenth century.

25. Thomas Richards puts it very well: "the pursuit of knowledge is the vanguard, not the rearguard of the pursuit of power" (5).

26. See D. A. Miller, Ronald Thomas, and Jon Thompson. Patrick Brantlinger does not focus on detective fiction per se, but his readings of some detective stories in *Rule of Darkness*, published the same year as *The Novel and the Police*, provide an excellent example of what I mean here. His reading of Taylor's *Confessions of a Thug*, a wildly popular crime novel that records the detective work of the Thug Police, cites this text as an instance of an imperialism always already confident in its reformist mission. He does not consider the state of policing both at home and abroad, which severely qualifies the kind of confidence on which his reading depends. Ed Wiltse has persuasively argued that Holmes criticism in particular has relied too heavily on applications of Foucault's theory of panopticism. See his "'So Constant an Expectation': Sherlock Holmes and Seriality."

27. Colquhoun was one of the first to press for an organized system of local knowledge: the police gazette. While Colquhoun was the first to think it through thoroughly, in doing so he rehabilitated an idea devised almost a half-century earlier by the Fielding

brothers. The gazette, ideally a national compendium of all criminal and police activity in various jurisdictions, made local knowledge a remedy for national security imperiled by Britain's imperial expansion. It is thus a snapshot of the detective narrative's larger logic that social order depended on making legible a rapidly expanding nation. See Thomas Richards's *The Imperial Archive* for an in-depth examination of how knowledge authorizes the fantasy of Empire. While Richards's argument about knowledge in the nation's service resonates with my claims about the detective, it is exemplary of the blind spots of genre studies that even though he considers two novels that revolve around detection, Kipling's *Kim* and Erskine Childers's *Riddle of the Sands,* he does not discuss the detective figure or the genre of detective fiction—presumably because he is discussing imperial fiction.

28. My sense of the detective, then, resonates with Colley's definition of nationalism: "Britishness was superimposed over an array of internal differences in response to contact with the Other, and above all in response to conflict with the Other" (6). Along similar lines, Poovey's *Making a Social Body* attempts to trace the "process of homogenization" in nation formation, which, she argues, "has not received as much attention recently as has the history of internal fragmentation" (2).

Notes to Chapter 1

1. See Linda Colley for a masterful discussion of how using France as an "obviously alien 'Them'" enabled England to draw the boundaries of its own national identity (6).

2. My use of the word *forgets* refers to Simon Gikandi's argument about the construction of English national identity in the nineteenth century. He describes how a "strategic forgetfulness" enables an elision of the colonial from what it means to be English (78). For an extended consideration of the "colonial dimension" of the emergence of the police, see the work of sociologist Mike Brogden.

3. See Ian Ousby for one of the most comprehensive discussions of *Caleb Williams* as a formative text in the emergence of the English detective novel. While Ousby's reading of detective fiction invaluably looks at its social function, it shares with other criticism of the genre an assumption that detective fiction is characteristically insular, distinct from other contemporaneous genres (gothic, picaresque) by virtue of its local focus. Detective fiction has been characterized by critics as a myopic tradition, at its most nearsighted a genre of ratiocinative puzzles or psychological journeys, and at its most farsighted a response to domestic social issues. Readings of *Caleb Williams* as a psychological game between Caleb and Falkland abound. Storch provides a classic example of the psychological approach to the genre. In response to such types of readings, Marilyn Butler argues that the domestic politics of the 1790s, specifically English aftershocks of the French Revolution, are central to Godwin's novel. Maurice Hindle's 1987 preface to the Penguin edition of the novel is a comprehensive introduction to the novel's relationship to the politics of the 1790s. Godwin is the original author of both interpretations. At the time of its writing, Godwin was careful to stress the novel's relationship to his political writings, adding that his intention in writing literature was a way of disseminating the political ideas expressed in *Political Justice* to a wider audience. His 1832 preface to *Fleetwood,* which focuses on the narrative elements of the

novel (for example, its famous backward construction), has opened the door for critics to argue that an apolitical interpretation of the novel is the one Godwin ultimately endorsed. See Marilyn Butler, 239–40. Many critics limit *Caleb Williams's* social criticism to indictments of the conditions of English prisons or the travesty of judicial proceedings in England. While these are obviously central to the novel, Godwin's writings around the time of *Caleb Williams* show that he does not see English problems as strictly English. Though Jon Thompson writes in the introduction to his *Fiction, Crime, and Empire* that *Caleb Williams* "inaugurated a way of evaluating society that has since become a convention of crime fiction" (2), his exclusion of Godwin's novel from any further consideration in his book, which is on the relationship between the crime fiction genre and Empire, illustrates how even thorough critical treatments of the novel tend to ignore its imperial context.

4. Mill's text, begun in 1805, was finished in 1817.

5. For a thorough account of the Hastings trial, see P. J. Marshall's *The Impeachment of Warren Hastings.* While the lengthy trial—which featured twenty-two charges and speeches by, in addition to Burke, Charles James Fox, Charles Grey, and Richard Brinsley Sheridan—defies summarization, the charges surrounded Hastings's misuse of his power as head of the East India Company. Four of the main charges, usefully summarized in Suleri's *The Rhetoric of English India,* related to the "rebellion" of Chait Singh, leader of Benares, and the Company's suppression of that rebellion; the violation of an agreement between the Company and the "Begums" of Oudh (the grandmother and mother of the underage Nawab), who, the Company claimed, helped support Chait Singh; the acceptance of bribes and presents by Hastings; and the wrongful granting of contracts for opium, military supplies, and emergency shipments of grain (210). Suleri's synopsis does not include the execution of Nuncomar, which I discuss later in this chapter; while it colored the whole trial, it was not one of the official charges against Hastings.

6. Godwin would add a note to the third edition of *Political Justice* describing Burke's fall from grace as "a memorable example, of the power of a corrupt system of government, to undermine and divert from their genuine purposes, the noblest faculties that have yet been exhibited to the observation of the world" (789).

7. See Stokes's and Stephen's earlier works of the same name, especially volume 2 on James Mill.

8. The radical tailor Francis Place, as E. P. Thompson (1966) points out, unites many of the diverse tendencies of reform politics within himself in addition to uniting diverse reformers. He was a close friend of both Godwin and Mill, as well as a friend of and fellow *Gorgon* editor with another radical reformer who will be discussed in this chapter, John Wade, whose *A Treatise on the Police and Crimes of the Metropolis* (1829) appears to concretize the terms for national acceptance of the police. Indicative of the strange bedfellows of reform politics, Place was an author of the "People's Charter," a savage critic of government despotism, and the designer of the "baton charge" of the police, which, with its restrained use of force, has come to signify what is uniquely English about the English police.

9. Dying in 1836, neither would have entirely endorsed the logic they helped put in motion. While I argue that they provide the basis, and Mill, if he had lived, would certainly have shown a Dickensian enthusiasm for the efficiency and local knowledge of the New Police, it is doubtful that even the increasingly liberal Godwin (who writes in an

1819 letter to Lady Caroline Lamb: "I am in principle a Republican, but in practice a Whig") would embrace the centralized midcentury police system (qtd in Peter Marshall 343). Godwin's connection to and distance from the middle class "counterrevolution" that followed the radical 1790s is apparent in E. P. Thompson's list of counterrevolutionaries: "Godwin giving way to Bentham, Bentham giving way to Malthus, M'Culloch and Dr. Ure, and these giving rise to Baines, Macaulay and Edwin Chadwick" (1966, 808).

10. See Myers, and Cobb.

11. My quotations from Godwin's Empire writings, unless otherwise specified, come from the Marken and Pollin collection.

12. Schevermann provides a close textual comparison of Godwin and Howard.

13. Gines, in doing the dirty work for Falkland, is attached to the decadent empire embodied by his boss. Not only is Falkland associated with extinct empires of Nero, Caligula, and Alexander, but he is literally decaying, like Dorian Gray, before the eyes of the reader. When he is brought into the courtroom at the conclusion of the novel, Caleb can hardly believe how physically decrepit his former master has become.

14. See McGowen (1986) for his consideration of Foucault's characterization of nineteenth-century English criminal law as a move away from offense (punishment) toward defense (such as prevention of crime, and investigation).

15. Nuncomar is the anglicization of Nanda Kumar. Even though the Nuncomar incident was not a part of the impeachment charges, it so enraged the prosecution that it colored the whole trial.

16. See Hutchins on Mill and administrative specialism (17).

17. In *Selected Writings*, ed. John Clive (Chicago: University of Chicago Press, 1972).

18. Indeed, Mill ultimately exonerates Hastings, explaining that in such a murky and criminal culture, it is hard to find the path of rectitude. Wilson notes this weak and contradictory move on Mill's part in his aforementioned defense of Hastings (4:369).

19. Though E. P. Thompson laments the progression toward "the ideology of the middle-class Utilitarians" demonstrated by Wade's later work, Thompson gives Wade credit for wrestling with the uneasy alliance between Utilitarianism and working-class radical politics (1966, 773).

20. This phrase is taken from B. Kirkman Gray's explanation of the 1800 act authorizing the first census of the English people (qtd. in Radzinowicz 1:35).

21. See Goodlad for a recent discussion of the "profound contradictions" in Victorian national character evident in both the expansion of the authority of the British state and "the notion of England's singular claims to freedom" (2000, 145).

22. McGowen writes that the early-nineteenth-century attack on gallows-style justice "proclaimed the dignity and value of human life," but it also "suggested the vulnerability of this life to assaults from those at odds with society. It thus increased dependence upon a state that protected one from violence" (1989, 142).

NOTES TO CHAPTER 2

1. Queen Victoria had a share in the production of Taylor's *Confessions of a Thug*, acquiring early proofs from the court publisher and urging the author toward brisk completion of his manuscript (Taylor 1986, 106).

2. Henry H. Spry, Sleeman's cousin and chief medical officer at the Jubbulpore Thug prison, was particularly interested in Thug phrenology and provided the skulls of seven convicted Thugs for a study by Robert Cox, who published a paper in the March 1834 Phrenological Journal.

3. For treatments of Thuggee that are informed by Foucault's theory of panopticism, see Brantlinger and David. There are numerous older hagiographic accounts by Sleeman's descendants and colleagues. Contemporary critics are becoming just as fascinated with the Thugs as were the Victorians. Notable recent work on Thuggee includes Martine van Woerkens's *The Strangled Traveler: Colonial Imaginings and the Thugs of India;* Parama Roy's *Indian Traffic,* particularly her chapter "Discovering India, Imagining Thuggee"; and Maire ni Fhlathuin's two excellent articles "'That Solitary Englishman': W. H. Sleeman and the Biography of British India" and "The Travels of M. De Thevenot: Through the Thug Archive."

4. Moslems were also Thugs, and this fact presented an interpretive difficulty for the English who were more comfortable understanding these groups as oppositional.

5. Thugs who operate on the river, fearful that stabbed bodies will leave blood upon the water, instead break all the spinal bones.

6. Maire ni Fhlathuin recently suggested to me that this quotation is actually from an anonymous (Sleeman-authored) letter to a newspaper that Parks copied into her text. I am grateful to Dr. ni Fhlathuin for her reading of this chapter.

7. And in fact this becomes the traditional argument for the eventual acceptance of policing at home, here described by Reith with his characteristic patriotic economy, "police principles are essentially the product of the character of the British people" (26).

8. Charles Trevelyan, in his review of Sleeman's *Ramaseeana,* an eight-volume work on the Thugs named for their special slang, suggests that he would be "much surprised" if the Thugs "should fail to rouse the attention of the most sluggish reader" (357). With the phenomenon of Thuggee, Trevelyan continues, readers are presented with something "more striking than anything that romancers have feigned touching the Old Man or the Mountain, or the Secret Tribunals of Germany" (357). This comparison is echoed in a *Literary Gazette* review of Taylor's novel: "The history of mankind affords no parallel to Thuggee: the bands of the Old Man of the Mountain scattered over many lands, the Secret Tribunals of Germany, the Inquisition, were all petty murderers, when compared with this terrible association" (466).

9. Bernard Porter suggests that this traditional distaste for spying is the reason a special branch for intelligence was not officially formed in England until 1887, when a colonial threat at home—the Fenians—called forth this new type of policing. Several scholars, from E. P. Thompson to some police historians, are quick to point out that while there was a public distrust of spies, the government always had the use of secret police, albeit in an extremely unsystematic manner.

10. This is very much the strategy of police reformers at home. Edwin Chadwick's 1829 article on "Preventive Police" begins with the point that

> some conspicuous portion of each day's recorded transactions adds to the impression on the public mind, that the introduction of a preventive system of police has become absolutely necessary. The public opinion cannot be too early or too fully matured by research and discussion on every part of the subject. (252)

Addressing the concerns of a reluctant public was the first priority of the early reformers, as well as the first commissioners, Rowan and Mayne. As a result, reformers were
"content not to ask for broad police powers" and the Commissioners especially were
vigilant both in monitoring and responding in writing to complaints in the daily
newspapers (Smith 33, 49).

11. This process demonstrates what Christopher Herbert has called the ethnographic idea of culture, and the methods of the Thug Police in the 1830s demonstrate precisely the type of science of observation Herbert suggests is then emerging
as Victorian protoethnography. Herbert describes how the ethnographic observer
reads "every customary practice" as participating in "a great self-enclosed system"
(194). The ethnographic idea of culture, Herbert explains, is that every small detail
stands in synecdochic relation to the whole culture. Similarly, the now allied read-
er/detective discovers that the story of India is to be found in the story of Thuggee;
each aspect of a Thug crime is not simply a part of a larger Thuggee system, but
indicative of the larger Indian culture. The alliance of the reader/detective also
demonstrates what will become a convention of detective fiction: The reader plays
detective as he follows, and indeed perhaps anticipates the deductions of the fictional
detective.

12. Peter Robb agrees that the efforts against dacoity led to the creation of the
Special Branch in 1887 (129).

13. See Lorhli.

14. See Jacobson for the most thorough account of the John Jasper-as-Thug
hypothesis (indeed the most thorough account of instances of Thuggee in English literature). Edmund Wilson is perhaps the most famous adherent to this position.

15. In other words, if Thuggee had not been "discovered," it would have had to
be invented. And according to Stewart Gordon, in large measure it was:

> it was the writing of William Sleeman and the Evangelical, crusading tone of the
> British Indian administration of the 1830s that played up these locally-orga-
> nized, small-scale marauding groups . . . into a hideous, widespread religious
> conspiracy, somehow typical of Indian and Indian "national character". (429)

While the actual nature of Thuggee—whether it be unsystematic local crime, as
Gordon suggests, or misunderstood religious practices or a nascent resistance movement to name simply a few perspectives—is obviously crucial to any proper understanding of the phenomenon (van Woerkens takes this question up in great detail in
The Strangled Traveler), it is beyond the scope of this argument, which is concerned
with the opportunity Thuggee, as represented by the British, provided the British for
"discovering" the detective. Thus it goes—almost—without saying that when I discuss the colonial police, I'm concerned with the British officers and not the native
forces. For a basic discussion of the organization of the Indian police in the nineteenth
and twentieth centuries, see Bayley, and for several considerations of both British and
native colonial forces, see Anderson and Killingray.

16. "Obsessive preoccupation with the problems of 'law and order,'" Basudev
Chatterji explains in an article on early-nineteenth-century policing in Bengal, is
"characteristic of the colonial rule in general" as it represents the justification for
British presence (38).

17. For similar concerns, see also Hervey (1: 79). An early-nineteenth-century "manual" for company servants written by A. F. Tytler illustrates the concern that the rogue cop is a problem abroad as well as at home; Tytler explains that "the character of Jonathan Wild is to be found in every Daroga" (qtd. Chatterji 39).

18. To be fair, authors such as Brantlinger and David treat Thuggee only briefly in their considerations of the literature of Empire, with David, for example, placing her reading within the interesting context of a larger British feminization of indigenous culture. See Stewart Gordon.

19. Of course it is impossible to determine the degree to which Sleeman's contemporaries, who emphasized these same qualities, shaped these subsequent nineteenth-century detectives, or whether twentieth-century descriptions of Sleeman, such as those by Griffiths, Tuker, and James Sleeman, are read back onto Sleeman post–Bucket/Holmes. While I think there is abundant evidence that the widely read representations of Sleeman and the Thug Police cast a mold for the type of detective dominant well into the twentieth century, the point is not (or not entirely) where this model originated but that the selling point of the detective, then and now, is his ability to balance sympathy with mastery, to reduce a culture to (or deduce a culture from) facts taken in by omnivorous yet compassionate eyes.

20. Biographer Sir Francis Tuker argues that if Sleeman's advocacy of a noninterventionist policy in Oudh had been taken seriously, the Mutiny could have been avoided.

21. While it is tempting to see Simmons making the same equation between a knowledge of Thuggee and a knowledge of "the vast Indian subcontinent," here he is talking about Taylor's novels as a whole, which cover a range of Anglo-Indian history, from his *Tippoo Sultan* (1840) about the Mysore War to *A Mahratta Tale* (1863) about the beginning of Mahratta rule in 1657 to *Seeta* (1872), a novel about an interracial love affair during the Mutiny. For a recent reading of Taylor's work, see Kapila.

22. The phrase comes from James Clifford's description of ethnography as a "hybrid textual activity: it traverses genres and disciplines" (26).

23. An 1839 review of the novel in *The Literary Gazette* explains that this "strange work, which is an authentic relation of those dreadful massacres brought to light by Colonel Sleeman and others, [is] only indebted to Captain Taylor for the interesting shape into which he has thrown his account of them" (466). Taylor biographer Mansukhani stresses that the result of Taylor's organizational efforts is something new:

> These incidents traced to their sources, mainly Sleeman and Thornton, go to show that Taylor was a great borrower, but in his work, ordinary incidents suffer a change into something rich and strange. Taylor does not merely reproduce what he finds in his sources. . . . What a vast difference between the plain and matter-of-fact account of Sleeman, and the gripping and pathetic story of Taylor! (115–16)

24. Holme writes, for example, that the "anxiety of the Indian Thugs to prevent their female relatives from becoming acquainted with the dreadful profession which they exercise, is attested by numerous passages in the Confessions of the Thug, Ameer Ali" (243–44).

25. See Philip Collins.

Notes to Chapter 3

1. *Bleak House* began its run in 1852, a year after Dickens's detective articles.

2. It took until 1842, thirteen years after the Metropolitan Police were established, for a small detective force (eight officers) to be formed. It was not until 1862 that regular plainclothes patrols were instituted (Radzinowicz 4: 189).

3. Samuel Smiles's article, "The Police of London," provides an example of this new view as it praises police conduct under the fire of Hyde Park rioters:

> The police behaved throughout with the greatest calmness and courage, as well as forbearance, notwithstanding that they themselves suffered serious bodily injuries. . . . caused by the bricks and stones that were hurled at them. . . . Perhaps in no other country but England would a powerful body of men, standing forward in defence of the law, have so long and so patiently submitted to be pelted, bruised and battered by a howling mob without being provoked into retaliation. (124–25)

4. The baton charge was Place's attempt to contain police violence.

5. See Philip Collins for a seminal work on Dickens's role in inventing and popularizing the Metropolitan Police. D. A. Miller characterizes Dickens's *Household Words* pieces as "apologetics for the new forces of order" (94). See also William Long's information-packed essay on Dickens and Inspector Field.

6. Hutter, Lambert, Symons, and Cawelti all discuss *The Moonstone* as the first English detective novel. Robinson writes of Cuff as having "fathered . . . a multitudinous progeny in the literature of detection" (220).

7. While this is obviously an important observation in the argument about Empire and detective fiction, it is indicative of a tradition that tends to ignore Empire, so that when it is discussed, it is discussed as romantic coloring. According to Julian Symons, *The Moonstone's* "implied contrast between the mysterious East and the humdrum reality of Victorian life, gives full play to Collins's subdued romanticism" (51). See also Cawelti (141).

8. These phrases are Simon Gikandi's. Many critics, naturally, see detective fiction as a way of "reading" society. According to an often cited article, Albert Hutter argues that "the police were needed to 'read' a city which had grown far beyond the easy knowledge of its inhabitants" (235). My sense of Dickens's and Collins's contributions differ from such critics in the nature of the society that they read.

9. The line is from Kipling's "The English Flag" (1990, 16–18).

10. See Pratt, Gikandi, Colley, and Baucom.

11. Dickens biographer, Edgar Johnson, reads *Drood* as a sign of Dickens's emerging anti-imperialism. DeWind, while reading *Drood* as a story of, albeit necessarily partial, reconciliation of East and West, calls Dickens "an ardent imperialist" (169). This sense of Dickens as on some level ambivalent about Empire characterizes most current criticism. Tambling writes "there is an ambiguity about his own complicity with the idea of imperialism" (173). See also David, Perera, and Said's *Culture and Imperialism*.

12. Such unawareness has been part of the definition of English imperialism since the nineteenth century. In a series of lectures given to Cambridge undergraduates in 1881–1882, J. R. Seeley (in)famously suggests that it is very English, "very characteristic" to "have conquered and peopled half the world in a fit of absence of mind" (12).

Seeley's point is not that Empire is actually accidental, but that the dominant representation of it is as such. Brantlinger argues that a certain dismissiveness is proof of the presence of imperialist feelings: "That the early and mid-Victorians did not call themselves imperialists . . . suggests merely that they did not feel self-conscious or anxious about their world domination" (23). This "unawareness" characterizes Collins's imperialism, as well, suggests Julian Wolfreys. "Part of such identity is a somewhat necessary lack of awareness," he writes, "A certain 'native' unawareness on Collins's part can be understood to stem from a confidence in a sense of national identity" (105).

13. Colley suggests that "by 'England,' they usually meant much more than just one part of the island they inhabited. The term became for them . . . a synonym for Great Britain as a whole and very often for its empire as well" (162).

14. Perhaps the blurring of these boundaries is best captured in *Drood*'s opening paragraph, in which Jasper's opium-obscured vision morphs an old English cathedral town into chaotic colonial pageantry.

15. Colley explains that in the contemporary English identity crisis over European unification, "apparent insularity is to be explained also by their growing doubts about who they are in the present" (375). Wolfreys accounts for this anxiety well: "If the imperial and colonial agendas are concerned with making other territories and other peoples English, then accompanying this is the fear that Englishness might be spread a little too thinly, its essence diluted, corrupted, lost" (31).

16. And here Dickens is like "nearly everyone in Britain [who] regarded this as a matter for national self-congratulation; one proof, among others, of liberal Britain's superiority over all other societies everywhere" (Porter 2). Social historians would both agree and disagree. Dickens's response *was* indicative of a middle-class celebration of liberal Britain's New Police, but as Robert Storch and others have shown, there was more resistance to these "reformed" police in the working class. It is interesting to note, however, that the terms of working-class resistance to the police are couched in the nationalist language that Dickens converts to propolice effect. One working-class leader wrote that "they must exercise their strength to put down this blue-bottle force, or this country will soon be like Venice, governed by a little band of tyrants" (qtd. in Storch 66). During antipolice disturbances, the police were told by working-class agitators to "Go home to your own country" (Storch 78).

17. The early 50s also found the end of the transportation of convicts to Australia, which promised the return of un-English Englishmen from the peripheries. That Dickens was concerned about the meaning of this return is evident in the character of Magwitch in *Great Expectations*.

18. Philip Thurmond Smith writes that

> The Great Exhibition . . . brought forth a strident crop of dire warnings to the authorities. In a letter to the Home Secretary, George Graham, an "aeronaut" [balloonist] . . . warned of 90,000 foreigners, 150,000 Irishmen and 60,000 Irishwomen, and assorted Chartists who were ready to join forces, and at a signal rise up and kill as many English as possible. (74)

19. Despite some criticism of Miller's strong reading, it is still the dominant way of reading Bucket. See Ronald Thomas's recent "Double Exposures" in which Bucket embodies the "positive version of panoptical social power" (100).

20. Indeed, Dickens, torn between the Scylla of his desires and the Charybdis of conventionality, famously delighted in Collins's iconoclasm. While it is more characteristic to see Dickens borrowing from the detective fiction of Collins, for example *Drood*'s obvious debt to *The Moonstone*, Ross Murfin argues that *The Moonstone* is an extension of the concerns of *Bleak House*.

21. See Nayder (1992), 216–18, for a reading of their different positions. I write "seeming" because there is very little material, other than "Perils of Certain English Prisoners," which Nayder discusses in her work *Unequal Partners*, to light on Collins's explicit attitudes toward both this event and another that evoked a strong response from Dickens, the Governor Eyre controversy. Collins scholars can only hope that the recent publication of a collection of his letters may partially illuminate his complicated politics.

22. According to Collins biographer Nuel Pharr Davis, Collins "had let himself misconstrue Dickens's instructions so far as to make" the leader of the uprising "the hero and the English prisoners a set of low comedians" (207).

23. In *Letters/Charles Dickens*, Madeline House and Graham Storey, eds. (1965–2002).

24. John R. Reed's essay is the work most often cited. I have already mentioned Ronald Thomas's work. See also Heller. For readings that generally argue that *The Moonstone* is a critique of imperialism, see Lonoff and Nayder. Both Roy and David read the novel more or less supporting imperial attitudes.

25. Taylor suggests that the separation of these two stories, the detective and the imperial, is borne out by the novel's structure. "The resolution of the double mystery," she writes, "is thus structurally separated from the return of the colonial plunder— the original crime—which takes place beyond the perimeters of the Story itself" (180). Winifred Hughes also reads the Indian story as setting up the limits of the detective story: "The prologue and the epilogue, set in the wilds of India and infused with the spirit of the Hindu religion, confirm the existence of realities beyond the reach of the detective, the appropriate emissary of modern rationality and legal sanctions" (164).

26. Elliot Gilbert writes of the "necessary failure of the detective" in *The World of Mystery Fiction* (1978). Gruner argues that Cuff's failure shows that "there are family secrets which the police cannot penetrate" (140). David's reading of the novel also posits Cuff as a failure (147).

27. And I would argue that he is central to wrapping up the specific investigation, interceding precisely at the moment where Blake is dropping the ball, that is, missing a crucial rendezvous with Gooseberry, the wide-eyed police prodigy. And once the red herring of Rachel has been removed (though certainly Cuff is validated in thinking she holds a crucial clue to solving the mystery), Cuff figures out the identity of the real culprit before he is, literally, unmasked.

28. See Nayder for a critique of Miller's use of Bakhtin (1992, 215).

29. My emphasis on Cuff and Murthwaite leaves out the character who is usually the focus of all other readings of *The Moonstone*'s imperial story: Ezra Jennings. Jennings's popularity in critical treatments of the novel stems perhaps from the unavoidable connection between this addicted, misunderstood outsider and the iconoclastic Collins, who wrote much of the novel through a pharmaceutical haze. Jennings, the mixed-race assistant to Dr. Candy and resident opium expert, is a cen-

tral detective figure. (One could certainly argue that Cuff plus Jennings, rather than Murthwaite, better measures up to that yardstick of English detectives, Sherlock Holmes: a drug-addicted scientific supersleuth.) There is nothing in these largely persuasive readings that substantially contradicts mine. Indeed, the story of the eventual acceptance of a figure, such as Jennings, whose un-English "appearance is against him" (359), resonates with the complicated history of the police in England. Jennings's colonial heritage underscores that English detectives are necessarily imperial figures. As a doctor, he shares his expert knowledge with an extended family in crisis. But the dominant critical emphasis on Jennings is unsatisfactory; it does not explain the importance of Betteredge as the main narrator, nor does it address why Jennings, by the novel's end, is buried along with his discoveries and Cuff and Murthwaite are at large, continuing to send explanatory missives to a still curious public. Casting a protopsychoanalyst as the sleuth too easily enables the type of reading, dominant in detective fiction criticism, that wants to read the genre as a private, psychological exercise.

30. While Cuff might represent a new kind of authority for a progressive modern era, Collins is careful to show him as equally at home with tradition, evident in his retirement "far from the crimes and the mysteries of the great city, [where] the illustrious thief-taker was placidly living out the last Sybarite years of his life, smothered in roses!" (397). As will another detective who retires to humble English hobbies in the countryside—Holmes and his beekeeping—Cuff chooses retirement "surrounded by the peaceful floricultural attractions of a country life" (451).

31. Roy describes Betteredge as the "leading player in the elaborate strategy protecting the text's sacrosanct English milieu" (660). While Betteredge is the figure for Englishness in this novel, in introducing the detective and his activity to the culture, he disrupts rather than protects.

32. David colorfully suggests that the "xenophobic" Betteredge "punctuat[es] his narrative with comical waves of the union jack" (17). Nayder, however, reads Betteredge as a transitional character, interestingly arguing that he plays both characters in his beloved *Crusoe,* Robinson and Friday (1992, 225–26).

33. This argument owes much to Pratt's observation that "the entity called Europe was constructed from the outside in as much as from the inside out" (6).

NOTES TO CHAPTER 4

1. This Strickland story was first published as No. 30, *Civil and Military Gazette,* 25 April 1887 and later became the short story "Miss Youghal's *Sais,*" and was collected in *Plain Tales from the Hills.* Strickland was based on an actual detective in the Punjab Police, John Paul Warbuton. According to Sir Percival Griffiths, an historian of the Indian Police, "It is generally believed that Warbuton was the model for Kipling's character of a police officer, Strickland, about whom he wrote in the *Civil and Military Gazette.* It is, at least, certain that Kipling met Warbuton and derived much of his knowledge of police matters from him" (405). In a connection that further suggests Kipling's work belongs in a history of detective fiction, rather than in a separate genre, Griffiths writes that Warbuton owes as much to Sleeman as Strickland does to him: "[Warbuton] followed what may be called the Sleeman method and having discovered

that the dacoits belonged to the Sansi tribe, he induced some of them to become approvers. Before long he had broken up the gang and restored peace to the country-side" (405). Strickland also bears a resemblance to Richard Burton. It has been fanta-sized in the pages of Sherlock fanzines that Burton was Holmes's traveling companion during his post-Reichenbach fall hiatus. See Pollock. That Burton could arguably be a model for Collins's explorer/detective Murthwaite, Kipling's Strickland, and a fanciful traveling companion for Holmes only further demonstrates the imbrication between the figures of the explorer and the detective.

2. The latter part of this quotation was in the original *Civil and Military Gazette* version, but was cut from the version included in *Plain Tales from the Hills*.

3. In arguing that both Kipling and Doyle create figures who redefine the nation, I am working against a trend of criticism that sees these two writers as the embodi-ment of a particularly insular nation. A recent article on Holmes's "otherness" by Ed Wiltse provides an excellent corrective to traditional Doyle criticism. See "'So Constant an Expectation': Sherlock Holmes and Seriality."

4. There are almost too many examples to mention, but see Said's introduction to *Kim*, and on Doyle, see Thomas (1994), Thompson, Lawrence Frank, and Joseph McLaughlin.

5. Jon Thompson importantly suggests that "rigid generic categories" tend "not only to obscure the hybrid nature of genres, but also to reduce literary analysis to the passing of arbitrary judgments" (4). And yet, Doyle and Kipling appear not only in separate chapters but in separate sections of his book. This separation leads to incon-sistencies in Thompson's otherwise very useful readings of these authors' works. In his chapter on Holmes, Thompson argues that Doyle "is able to create a form that natu-ralizes and hence supports English domination over India" (72), but pages later in his chapter on Kipling, he suggests that the spy genre distinguishes itself from the more insular detective genre by having the detective function take on "a 'world-historical' significance." He writes that "it is no longer just the fates of individuals that are at risk, but, in the case of England, and English literature, the fate of a proud imperial nation" (85).

6. It is Thompson's point that Doyle uses the genre to "push to the margins" potentially disruptive subjects, such as imperialism (68). Symons complains that the problems with Doyle's first two Holmes novels, *A Study in Scarlet* and *The Sign of the Four,* is that "detection is suspended" to make room for historical adventure and imperial intrigue (64–65). See John Cawelti's standard account of popular genre fic-tion *Adventure, Mystery, and Romance: Formula Stories as Art and Popular Culture* for an example of the categorical imperative in genre studies. Joseph McLaughlin quotes from the introduction to a recent edition of Holmes, written by detective writer Loren Estleman, that encourages "those who prefer their Sherlock Holmes served up pure and without digression" should skip the non-England parts of *A Study in Scarlet* (36–37).

7. It is beyond the scope of this book to investigate thoroughly both the reasons for and implications of this division between detective and spy fiction. While I hope to continue this inquiry in a subsequent project, it is my working hypothesis that this critical distinction retroactively produces the divisions understood to be the reasons for it in the first place. One of the central characteristics distinguishing spy fiction from detective fiction is the former's allegedly broader and, therefore, more disillu-

sioned and more politicized understanding of the world. But as this characterization ignores the political nature of the debate about the character of English imperial authority at the heart of detective fiction, it leads to critical acrobatics. For example, Doyle's later stories are criticized for putting aside detection and engaging in themes more appropriate for gothic or espionage tales (Ousby 170–71). Symons quotes a critic describing Conrad's *The Secret Agent* as a "political detective novel" (217) and writes that Anthony Boucher "remarked on the wave of British patriotism which 'led almost every top-flight mystery writer to save the Empire from Fascism by the intervention of his star detective'" (222). The critical forgetting of detective fiction's political past is most clear in the divisions within the spy tradition. Critical assessments such as Symons's that "after the First World War began, spy stories became unequivocally nationalist in tone and right-wing in political sympathy" (218) and Jon Thompson's that *Kim* is the precursor "to the romantic and heroic" spy tradition and Conrad's *The Secret Agent* to the critical or ironic" tradition (86) ignore that detective stories articulate an emergent nationalism from the beginning of the century and that detective novels, like *Confessions of a Thug* (1839) or *The Moonstone* (1868), contain within them perspectives on national authority ranging from heroic to ironic. Indeed, it is the founding premise of this work that the history of the detective in England is better understood in terms of that figure's *necessity* rather than that figure's heroism, a distinction that underscores how critiques of authority produce new authorities.

8. This argument is also paradoxical in that Ousby suggests elsewhere that Holmes himself becomes less exotic and more refined, that is moves away from the outré bohemianism of the early stories, as he gets older.

9. This logic is explained well by Gerald Newman:

> England's past cultural interpreters, many of them, were so influenced by national myths that we ourselves, inheriting their concepts, have not quite yet gotten so far above these myths as to be able to understand their multifarious workings—to see, for example, how they still affect our own vision, and to see also how, as all-embracing historic ideological phenomena, they underlay and secretly imparted hidden directionality to the particular events and movement we ordinarily study and write about. (xix)

10. She suggestively continues "in part imitating Conan Doyle's ability to illuminate and transform the ordinary details of life, detective novelists liberally sprinkle charts, diagrams, timetables, maps, plans and other concrete evidence throughout their books, indicating the English tradition of empirical thought" (101).

11. See Cailois, and Marcus. This is a surprisingly persistent reading. See Rosemary Jann (53).

12. Famous Marxist accounts of the genre, such as Franco Moretti's or Ernst Mandel's, argue that detective fiction is an agent of conservative ideology that makes crime and its solution the province of unique, or uniquely disturbed, individuals, rather than the responsibility of society. Critics such as Jon Thompson, Thomas, and Jann share with D. A. Miller's dominant Foucauldian reading of detective fiction an understanding of the genre as working toward order by policing resistance or difference, or both. Wiltse again provides an important perspective on this tradition. He writes that the Holmes stories

have been seen as both a cause and an effect of the triumph of the carceral society, and Holmes has been read repeatedly as the ideal surveillant in that society,
a kind of *ur*-policeman who is all the more effective in his disciplinary function
for being separate from the official police. However, Foucauldian readings of
Holmes have consistently failed to account for the degree to which he is himself
on many of the boundaries of bourgeois normality he has been assumed to patrol.
(107)

13. Other Holmes stories commonly cited as espionage narratives are "The Naval
Treaty," "The Second Stain," and "His Last Bow."

14. Owen Dudley Edwards's notes to the Oxford Sherlock Holmes support this
reading: "ACD uses Mycroft as a means to deplore the absence of such specialism co-
ordination in real life. The British official convention that 'foreign affairs' was a specialization (and rather a disreputable one) is also under fire" (184).

15. The definitions of "polyphony" and "motet" come from *Webster's Ninth New
Collegiate Dictionary.*

16. Ousby reads this as an innocuous version of the Aesthetic Movement's motto
of *art for art's sake,* in that the later Holmes is moving away from his counterculture
aesthete persona. But it clearly conjures up images of the Great Game, as well (159).

17. This characterization of London is echoed in many contemporary articles on
the police. Sir Charles Warren, a police commissioner, explains:

> London has for many years past been subject to the sinister influence of a mob
> stirred up into spasmodic action by restless demagogues. Their operation have
> exercised undue influence on the Government of the day, and year by year the
> Metropolis of our Empire has become more and more prone to dangerous pan-
> ics, which, if permitted to increase in intensity, must certainly lead to disastrous
> consequences. (577)

Warren continues in his article to argue for the necessity of the detective in order to
avert such "disastrous consequences."

18. What I mean to suggest here is that detective work actually redraws boundaries, as Richards suggests of Kipling's Kim, who "works within the domain not of
actual but of potential borders" (28). The global nature of this authority stands in contrast to the range of other authorities; in "The Mark of the Beast," Kipling's policeman, Strickland, demonstrates his power "East of Suez," where "the Church of
England Providence only exercis[es] an occasional and modified supervision in the
case of Englishmen" (1920b, 170). See Ousby for a discussion of the detective as an
agent of Providence.

19. Richards uses Deleuze and Guattari's idea of "nomadology" to read Kipling's
Kim as "the first sustained narrative of state nomadology" (23). Kim, like Deleuze and
Guattari's nomads, embodies all knowledge and yet rather than resisting the state, uses
them in the nation's service. See Richards's *The Imperial Archive,* particularly 19–32.

20. Doyle makes this point again and again, here in *The Hound of the Baskervilles.*
He tells Watson, who is smarting from having been kept from Holmes's investigation
on the Moor: "Our researches have evidently been running on parallel lines, and when
we unite our results I expect we shall have a fairly full knowledge of the case" (91).

21. See Said's introduction to the Penguin edition of *Kim*.

22. While the stakes are not as high in "Miss Youghal's *Sais*," Strickland's ability to impersonate a native *sais* enables him to win back his love interest and future wife, Miss Youghal. And while some could see Strickland's marriage as yet another instance of detective fiction's domestication of the imperial—he cannot go Fantee as a married man—it is actually the reverse. This union produces a son who continues the work of Empire; Adam Strickland's adventures—and travails—in Africa are the subject of the story "A Deal in Cotton." The narrator, a colleague of Strickland's, explains "our India laid aside—we talked Adam's Africa" (189).

23. Brantlinger captures the paradox in his statement that "the creator of that great incarnation of scientific rationalism Sherlock Holmes devoted himself to the spiritualist movement" (252). Brantlinger's chapter on imperial Gothic in his seminal *Rule of Darkness* is as tantalizing for the connections it does not make as much as for the ones it does, and of course it is unreasonable to ask him to consider more texts than the countless ones he discusses. It was the preponderance of what I consider to be detective narratives (Kipling's "Mark of the Beast," "The Return of Imray," Robert Louis Stevenson's *Dr. Jekyll and Mr. Hyde,* and Doyle's short stories) in the imperial Gothic chapter that got me thinking about detective stories as imperial narratives and the problem of critical partition.

24. See note 10.

25. The full quotation he is referencing is "There are more things in heaven and earth, Horatio, /Than are dreamt of in your philosophy."

NOTES TO CHAPTER 5

1. David Cannadine discusses a similar critical tendency in the work of historians in the preface to his *Ornamentalism:*

> The history of the British Empire is still all too often written as if it were completely separate and distinct from the history of the British nation. Those old-style historians who stressed metropolitan impulses, be they economic, military, moral or constitutional, tended to take Britain for granted, and to have very unnuanced notions of the metropolitan economy, society and polity from whence these emanations originated. And those more recent scholars who concentrate on the imperial periphery or work with texts and discourse tend to disregard Britain—either because they want to minimize the part the imperial metropolis played in the longer history of their nation or community, or (alternatively and contradictorily) because they prefer to settle for a cardboard caricature of British omnipotence and imperial wickedness. (xvii)

2. The phrase is from P. D. Morgan's "Encounters between British and 'Indigenous' Peoples, c. 1500–1800," which provides one of the epigraphs to Cannadine's *Ornamentalism.* I provide the full quotation here as it corresponds with my aim in this examination of the detective figure in literature:

> The real challenge . . . will be to . . . integrate the local and the general . . . Only then will we glimpse whole worlds . . . that have not been seen before. A synoptic

view, bringing metropole and colony, colonizer and colonized, British and indigenous peoples into one frame, into a single analytical field, will reveal not merely a catalogue of differences and similarities, not just a series of intriguing parallels, but whole configurations, general processes, an entire interactive system, one vast interconnected world. (68)

3. See Franco Moretti, "Clues," in *Signs Taken for Wonders*.

4. I am thinking here of the term as it is used in psychoanalytic theory, beginning with Joan Riviere's idea of "Womanliness as a Masquerade," in *Psychoanalysis and Female Sexuality*, 209–20.

WORKS CITED

Altick, Richard. 1986. *Deadly encounters: Two Victorian sensations.* Philadelphia: University of Pennsylvania Press.

Anon. 1802. *An address to the magistrates and people of Great Britain and Ireland, occasioned by the alarming system of modern imprisonment.* London: J. Ridgway.

Anderson, Benedict. 1991. *Imagined communities: Reflections on the origin and spread of nationalism.* New York: Verso.

Anderson, David M., and David Killingray, eds. 1991. *Policing the empire: Government, authority and control, 1830–1940.* New York: Manchester University Press.

Arac, Jonathan, and Harriet Ritvo, eds. 1995. Introduction to *Macropolitics of nine-tenth-century literature: Nationalism, exoticism, imperialism.* Durham: Duke University Press.

Armstrong, Nancy, and Leonard Tennenhouse, eds. 1989. Introduction to *The violence of representation: Literature and the history of violence.* New York: Routledge.

Arnold, David. 1994. The colonial prison: Power, knowledge and penology in nine-teenth century India. In *Subaltern studies VIII: Essays in honour of Ranajit Guha,* edited by David Arnold and David Hardiman. New Delhi: Oxford University Press.

Auden, W. H. 1988. The guilty vicarage. In *Detective fiction: A collection of critical essays,* edited by Robin Winks, 15–24. Woodstock, VT: Foul Play Press.

Baucom, Ian. 1999. *Out of place: Englishness, empire, and the locations of identity.* Princeton: Princeton University Press.

Bayley, David H. 1969. *The police and political development in India.* Princeton: Princeton University Press.

Bhabha, Homi K., ed. 1990. Introduction to *Nation and narration.* New York: Routledge.

Bond, E. A., ed. 1859–1861. Introduction to *Speeches of the managers and counsel in the trial of Warren Hastings.* 4 vols. London: Longman.

Brantlinger, Patrick. 1988. *Rule of darkness: British literature and imperialism, 1830–1914.* Ithaca: Cornell University Press.

Brogden, Mike. 1987a. An act to colonise the internal lands of the island: Empire and the origins of the professional police. *International Journal of the Sociology of Law* 15: 179–208.

———. 1987b. The Emergence of the police—the colonial dimension. *The British Journal of Criminology* 27, 1 (Winter): 4–22.

Buchan, John. 1994. *The thirty-nine steps.* New York: Dover.

Butler, Judith. 1990. *Gender trouble: Feminism and the subversion of identity.* New York: Routledge.

Butler, Marilyn. 1982. Godwin, Burke, and *"Caleb Williams." Essays in Criticism: A Quarterly Journal* 32, 3 (July): 237–57.

Caillois, Roger. 1983. The detective novel as game. In *The poetics of murder: Detective fiction and literary theory,* edited by Glenn W. Most and William W. Stowe, 1–12. New York: Harcourt Brace Jovanovich.

Cambridge guide to literature in English, The. 1988. Edited by Ian Ousby. Cambridge: Cambridge University Press.

Cannadine, David. 2001. *Ornamentalism: How the British saw their empire.* New York: Oxford University Press.

Carlyle, Thomas. 1850. Model prisons. In *Latter-day pamphlets.* New York: Harper and Brothers.

Cawelti, John. 1976. *Adventure, mystery, and romance: Formula stories as art and popular culture.* Chicago: University of Chicago Press.

Chadwick, Edwin. 1829. Preventive Police. *London Review,* 252–307.

Chatterji, Basudev. 1981. The darogah and the countryside: The imposition of police control in Bengal and its impact (1793–1837). *The Indian Economic and Social History Review* 18, 1: 19–42.

Claussen, Christopher. 1984. Sherlock Holmes, order and the late-Victorian mind. *Georgia Review* 38: 104–23.

Clifford, James, and George E. Marcus, eds. 1986. *Writing culture: The poetics and politics of ethnography.* Berkeley: University of California Press.

Cobb, Joann P. 1973. Godwin's novels and *"Political justice." Enlightenment Essays* 4: 15–28.

Colley, Linda. 1992. *Britons: Forging the nation: 1707–1837.* New Haven: Yale University Press.

Collins, Philip. 1994. *Dickens and crime.* New York: St. Martin's.

Collins, Wilkie. 1991. *The moonstone.* New York: Oxford University Press.

Colquhoun, Patrick. 1797. *A treatise on the police of the metropolis.* London: H. Fry.

———. 1818. *Considerations on the means of affording profitable employment to the redundant population of Great Britain and Ireland, through the medium of an improved and correct system of colonization in the British territories in South Africa.* London.

Critchley, T. A. 1970. *The conquest of violence: Order and liberty in Britain.* New York: Schocken Books.

David, Deirdre. 1995. *Rule Britannia: Women, empire, and Victorian writing.* Ithaca: Cornell University Press.

Davis, Nuel Pharr. 1956. *The life of Wilkie Collins.* Urbana: University of Illinois Press.

DeWind, John S. 1993. The empire as metaphor: England and the East in *"The mystery of Edwin Drood."* In *Victorian Literature and Culture,* edited by John Maynard and Adrienne Munich, vol. 21, 169–89. New York: AMS Press.

DePorte, Michael. 1984. The consolations of fiction: Mystery in *"Caleb Williams." Papers on Language and Literature* 20, 2 (Spring):154–64.

Dickens, Charles. 1850a. Detective police, The. *Household Words* 1.

———. 1850b. Modern science of thief-taking, The. *Household Words* (July 13): 368–72.

———. 1850c. On duty with Inspector Field. *Household Words* 1.

———. 1850d. Three "detective" anecdotes. *Household Words* 1.

——. 1853. Down with the tide. *Household Words* 1: 481–85.

——. 1868. The ruffian. In *The works of Charles Dickens,* Cleartype Edition. New York: Books, Inc.

——. 1968. The metropolitan protectives. Written with W. H. Wills. In *Charles Dickens's uncollected writings from* Household Words, *1850–1859,* edited by Harry Stone, 253–73. Bloomington: Indiana University Press.

——. 1972. *The mystery of Edwin Drood.* New York: Oxford University Press.

——. 1984. *Bleak house.* New York: Penguin.

——. n.d. The Niger expedition. In *Miscellaneous papers.* London: MacDonald and Sons.

Doyle, Arthur Conan. 1887. *A study in scarlet.* Cambridge: Cambridge University Press.

——. 1977. A scandal in Bohemia. In *Adventures of Sherlock Holmes.* New York: Ballantine.

——. 1994a. Adventure of the Bruce-Partington plans, The. In *His last bow.* New York: Oxford University Press.

——. 1994b. Cardboard box, The. In *The memoirs of Sherlock Holmes.* New York: Oxford University Press.

——. 1994c. Greek interpreter, The. In *The memoirs of Sherlock Holmes.* New York: Oxford University Press.

——. 1994d. His last bow. In *His last bow.* New York: Oxford University Press.

——. 1994e. *The hound of the Baskervilles.* New York: Dover.

——. 1994f. Naval treaty, The. In *The memoirs of Sherlock Holmes.* New York: Oxford University Press.

——. 1994g. Second stain, The. In *The return of Sherlock Holmes.* New York: Oxford University Press.

——. 1994h. *Sign of the four, The.* New York: Oxford University Press.

Eliot, T. S. 1951. Wilkie Collins and Dickens. In *Selected essays.* London: Faber and Faber.

Emsley, Clive. 1991. *The English police: A political and social history.* New York: St. Martin's.

Fanon, Frantz. 1967. *Black skin, white masks,* trans. Charles Lam Markmann. New York: Grove Press, Inc.

Fhlathuin, Maire ni. 2001. "That solitary Englishman": W. H. Sleeman and the biography of British India. *Victorian Review* 27, 1.

——. 2001. The travels of M. De Thevenot: Through the Thug archive. *The Journal of the Royal Asiatic Society* 11, 1.

Foucault, Michel. 1979. *Discipline and punish: The birth of the prison.* New York: Vintage.

Frank, Lawrence. 1996. Dreaming the medusa: Imperialism, primitivism, and sexuality in Arthur Conan Doyle's *"The sign of the four." Signs* 22, 1 (Autumn): 52–85.

Freitag, Sandra B. 1985. Collective crime and authority in North India. In *Crime and criminality in British India,* edited by Anand Yang, 140–56. Tucson: University of Arizona Press.

Galbraith, John Kenneth. 1968. Introduction to *The history of British India,* by James Mill. 6 vols. Fifth Edition. Edited by Horace Hayman Wilson. New York: Chelsea House.

Gikandi, Simon. 1996. *Maps of Englishness: Writing identity in the culture of colonialism.* New York: Columbia University Press.

Gilbert, Elliot. 1990. *The world of mystery fiction.* Bowling Green, OH: Bowling Green State University Popular Press.

Godwin, William. 1985. *Enquiry concerning political justice.* New York: Penguin Classics.

———. 1988. *Caleb Williams.* New York: Penguin Books.

Goodlad, Lauren M. E. 2000. "A middle class cut into two": Historiography and Victorian national character. *English Literary History* (hereinafter *ELH*) 67: 143–78.

———. 2003. Beyond the panopticon: Victorian Britain and the critical imagination. *Publications of the Modern Language Association of America* 118, 3: 539–56.

Gordon, Stewart N. 1969. Scarf and sword: Thugs, marauders, and state-formation in 18th century Malwa. *The Indian Economic and Social History Review* 4, 4: 403–29.

Griffiths, Sir Percival. 1971. *To guard my people: The history of the Indian police.* London: Ernest Benn.

Gruner, Elisabeth Rose. 1993. Family secrets and the mysteries of *"The moonstone."* In *Victorian literature and culture,* vol. 21, edited by John Maynard and Adrienne Munich, 127–45. New York: AMS Press.

Handwerk, Gary. 1993. Of Caleb's guilt and Godwin's truth: Ideology and ethics in *"Caleb Williams." ELH* 60, 4 (Winter): 939–60.

Harvey, A. D. 1976. The nightmare of *"Caleb Williams." Essays in Criticism* 26: 236–49.

Hay, Douglas. 1975. Property, authority and the criminal law. In *Albion's fatal tree: Crime and society in eighteenth-century England,* edited by Douglas Hay, et al. New York: Pantheon.

Heller, Tamar. 1992. *Dead secrets: Wilkie Collins and the female gothic.* New Haven: Yale University Press.

Herbert, Christopher. 1991. *Culture and anomie: Ethnographic imagination in the nineteenth century.* Chicago: University of Chicago Press.

Hervey, Charles. 1892. *Some records of crime.* 2 vols. London: Sampson Low, Marston & Company.

Hindle, Maurice. 1988. Introduction to *Caleb Williams,* by William Godwin. New York: Penguin Books.

Hobsbawm, Eric. 1969. *Bandits.* London: George Weidenfeld and Nicholson.

———. 1995. *Nations and nationalism since 1780: Programme, myth, reality.* New York: University of Cambridge Press.

Holme, Frederick. 1841. The secret societies of Asia—The assassins and thugs. *Blackwood's Magazine* 49 (February): 229–44.

Holquist, Michael. 1983. Whodunit and other questions: Metaphysical detective stories in postwar fiction. In *The poetics of murder: Detective fiction and literary theory,* edited by Glenn W. Most and William W. Stowe, 154–73. New York: Harcourt Brace Jovanovich.

Horwood, Sir William T. F. 1933. Foreword to *Thug or a million murders,* by James L. Sleeman, v–vii. London: Sampson Low, Marston.

House, Madeline, and Graham Storey, eds. *Letters/Charles Dickens* (Oxford: Clarendon Press, 1965–2002).

Howard, John. 1777. *The state of the prisons in England and Wales, with preliminary observations and an account of some foreign prisons.* Warrington: William Eyre.

Hughes, Robert. 1988. *The fatal shore: The epic of Australia's founding.* New York: Random House.

Hughes, Winifred. 1980. *The maniac in the cellar: Sensation novels of the 1860s.* Princeton: Princeton University Press.

Humphreys, Anne. 1991. Generic strands and urban twists: The Victorian mysteries novel. *Victorian Studies* 34, 4 (Summer): 455–72.

Hutchins, Francis. 1967. *The illusion of permanence: British imperialism in India.* Princeton: Princeton University Press.

Hutter, Albert D. 1983. Dreams, transformations, and literature: The implications of detective fiction. In *The poetics of murder: Detective fiction and literary theory,* edited by Glenn W. Most and William W. Stowe, 231–50. New York: Harcourt Brace Jovanovich.

Ignatieff, Michael. 1978. *A just measure of pain: The penitentiary in the industrial revolution, 1750–1850.* New York: Pantheon.

Jacobsen, Wendy. 1977. John Jasper and Thuggee. *The Modern Language Review* 72, 3: 526–37.

Jann, Rosemary. 1995. *The adventures of Sherlock Holmes: Detecting social order.* New York: Twayne Publishers.

Jeffries, Charles. 1952. *The colonial police.* London: Max Parrish.

Johnson, Barbara. 1987. *A world of difference.* Baltimore: Johns Hopkins University Press.

Kapila, Shuchi. 1998. Educating Seeta: Philip Meadows Taylor's romances of empire. *Victorian Studies* 41, 2 (Winter): 211–41.

Kipling, Rudyard. 1920a. A deal in cotton. In *The writings in prose and verse of Rudyard Kipling.* Vol. 20. New York: Scribner.

——. 1920b. Mark of the beast, The. In *The writings in prose and verse of Rudyard Kipling.* Vol. 4. New York: Scribner.

——. 1920c. Return of Imray, The. In *The writings in prose and verse of Rudyard Kipling.* Vol. 4. New York: Scribner.

——. 1987. Miss Youghal's *sais.* In *Plain tales from the hills.* New York: Penguin.

——. 1989. *Kim.* New York: Penguin.

——. 1990. *Rudyard Kipling: Gunga Din and Other Favorite Poems.* New York: Dover Publications, Inc.

Knight, Stephen. 1980. *Form and ideology in crime fiction.* Bloomington: Indiana University Press.

Lambert, Gavin. 1988. The dangerous edge. In *Detective fiction: A collection of critical essays,* edited by Robin Winks, 47. Woodstock, VT: Foul Play Press.

Lindeborg, Ruth. 1994. The "Asiatic" and the boundaries of Victorian Englishness. *Victorian Studies* 37: 381–404.

Lohrli, Anne. 1980. Charles Dickens and Philip Meadows Taylor. *Notes and Queries* (June): 211.

Long, William. 1987. The "Singler stories" of Inspector Field. *The Dickensian* 83, 3 (Autumn): 149–62.

Lonoff, Sue. 1982. *Wilkie Collins and his Victorian readers: A study in the rhetoric of authorship.* New York: AMS Press.

Low, Donald A. 1982. *Thieves' kitchen: The regency underworld.* Toronto: J. M. Dent.

Macaulay, Thomas Babington. 1928. Essay on Warren Hastings. Edited by Margaret J. Frick. London: Macmillan.

———. 1952. The Government of India. In *Macaulay: Prose and poetry*, edited by G. M. Young, 688–718. Cambridge: Harvard University Press.

———. n.d. Notes on the Indian penal code. In *The miscellaneous works of Lord Macaulay*, vol. 7. Edited by Lady Hannah Moremacaulay Trevelyan. New York: Putnam.

Mainwaring, George B. 1821. *Observations on the present state of the police of the metropolis*. London: John Murray.

Mandel, Ernest. 1988. A Marxist interpretation of the crime story. In *Detective fiction: A collection of critical essays*, edited by Robin Winks, 209–19. Woodstock, VT: Foul Play Press.

Mansukhani, Gobind Singh. 1951. *Philip Meadows Taylor: A critical study*. Bombay: New Book Co.

Marcus, Steven. Dashiell Hammet. In Most and Stowe, 197–209.

Marken, Jack W., and Burton R. Pollin, eds. 1968. *Uncollected writings by William Godwin*. Gainesville, FL: Scholars' Facsimiles and Reprints.

Marshall, Peter H. 1984. *William Godwin*. New Haven: Yale University Press.

Marshall, P. J. 1965. *The impeachment of Warren Hastings*. New York: Oxford University Press.

McCracken, David. 1970. Godwin's reading in Burke. *English Language Notes* (June): 264–70.

McGowan, Randall. 1986. A powerful sympathy: Terror, the prison, and humanitarian reform in early-nineteenth-century Britain. *Journal of British Studies* 25 (July): 312–34.

———. 1989. Punishing violence, sentencing crime. In *The violence of representation: Literature and the history of violence*, edited by Nancy Armstrong and Leonard Tennenhouse, 140–56. New York: Routledge.

McLaughlin, Joseph. 2000. *Writing the urban jungle: Reading empire in London from Doyle to Eliot*. Charlottesville: University of Virginia Press.

Mill, James. 1968. *The history of British India*. 6 volumes. Fifth Edition. Edited by Horace Hayman Wilson. New York: Chelsea House.

Miller, D. A. 1988. *The novel and the police*. Berkeley: University of California Press.

Mitchell, Timothy. 1992. Orientalism and the exhibitionary order. In *Colonialism and culture*, edited by Nicholas B. Dirks, 293–312. Ann Arbor: University of Michigan Press.

Moretti, Franco. 1988. *Signs taken for wonders: Essays in the sociology of literary forms*. New York: Verso.

———. 2000. The slaughterhouse of literature. *Modern Language Quarterly* 61, 1 (March): 207–27.

Morgan, P. D. 1999. Encounters between British and "indigenous" peoples, c. 1500–c. 1800. In *Empire and others: British encounters with indigenous peoples, 1600–1850*.

Most, Glenn W., and William W. Stowe, eds. 1983. *The poetics of murder: Detective fiction and literary theory*. New York: Harcourt Brace Jovanovich.

Mudimbe, V. Y. 1988. *The invention of Africa: Gnosis, philosophy, and the order of knowledge*. Bloomington: Indiana University Press.

Murfin, Ross. 1982. The art of representation: Collins' *"The moonstone"* and Dickens' *"Example." ELH* 49, 3 (Fall): 653–72.

Myers, Mitzi. 1972. Godwin's changing conception of *"Caleb Williams." SEL: Studies in English Literature* 12: 591–628.

Nayder, Lillian. 1992. Robinson Crusoe and Friday in Victorian Britain: Discipline, dialogue, and Collins's critique of empire in *"The moonstone." Dickens Studies Annual* 21: 213–31.

_____. 2002. *Unequal partners: Charles Dickens, Wilkie Collins, and Victorian authorship.* Ithaca: Cornell University Press.

Neal, David. 1991. *The rule of law in a penal colony: Law and power in early New South Wales.* New York: Cambridge University Press.

Newman, Gerald. 1987. *The rise of English nationalism: A cultural history, 1740–1830.* New York: St. Martin's.

O'Brien, Conor Cruise, ed. 1986. *Reflections on the revolution in France.* New York: Penguin.

——. 1989. Warren Hastings in Burke's great melody. In *The impeachment of Warren Hastings,* edited by Geoffrey Carnall and Colin Nicholson.

O'Brien, W. 1852. The police system of London. *Edinburgh Review* 96 (July): 1–3x.

O'Connor, Erin. 2003. Preface for a post-postcolonial criticism. *Victorian Studies* 45, 2 (Winter): 217–46.

Ousby, Ian. 1976. *Bloodhounds of heaven: The detective in English fiction from Godwin to Doyle.* Cambridge: Harvard University Press.

Page, Norman, ed. 1974. *Wilkie Collins: The critical heritage.* Boston: Routledge & Kegan Paul.

Parks, Fanny. 1850. *The wanderings of a pilgrim in search of the picturesque, during four and-twenty years in the East.* 2 vols. London: Pelham Richardson

Pendergast, Tom, and Sara Pendergast, eds. 2004. *The encyclopedia of the Victorian era.* 4 vols. James Eli Adams, editor-in-chief. Danbury, CT: Grolier Academic Press.

Perera, Suvendrini. 1991. *Reaches of empire: The English novel from Edgeworth to Dickens.* New York: Columbia University Press.

Plamenatz, John. 1958. *The English utilitarians.* Oxford: Basil Blackwell.

Pollock, Donald. 1975. Notes on a journey to Lhassa and Mecca. *The Baker Street Journal: An Irregular Quarterly of Sherlockiana* 25: 71–73.

Poovey, Mary. 1995. *Making a social body: British cultural formation, 1830–1869.* Chicago: University of Chicago Press.

Porter, Bernard. 1987. *The origins of the vigilant state: The London Metropolitan Police special branch before the First World War.* London: Weidenfeld and Nicolson.

Pratt, Mary Louise. 1992. *Imperial eyes: Travel writing and transculturation.* New York: Routledge.

Radzinowicz, Leon. 1948–1968. *History of English criminal law.* 4 vols. London: Stevens and Sons.

Reed, John R. 1973. English imperialism and the unacknowledged crime of *"The moonstone." CLIO: An Interdisciplinary Journal* 2, 3: 281–90.

Reith, Charles. 1943. *British police and the democratic ideal.* New York: Oxford University Press.

Review of *"Confessions of a Thug."* 1839. *Literary Gazette; and Journal of the Belles Lettres, Arts, Sciences, & C.* 27 July: 466–71.

Richards, Thomas. 1993. *The imperial archive: Knowledge and the fantasy of empire.* New York: Verso.

Riviere, Joan. 1966. Womanliness as a masquerade. In *Psychoanalysis and female sexuality,* edited by Henkrik M. Ruitenbeek. New Haven: College and University Press.

Robb, Peter. 1991. The ordering of rural India: The policing of nineteenth-century Bengal and Bihar. In *Policing the empire: Government, authority and control, 1830–1940,* edited by David M. Anderson and David Killingray, 126–47. New York: Manchester University Press.

Robinson, Kenneth. 1972. *Wilkie Collins, a biography.* Westport, CT: Greenwood Press.

Ross, Marlon B. 1995. Romancing the nation-state: The poetics of romantic nationalism. In *Macropolitics of nineteenth-century literature: Nationalism, exoticism, imperialism,* edited by Jonathan Arac and Harriet Ritvo, 56–85. Durham: Duke University Press.

Rowse, A. L. 1961. Macaulay's essays. In *Victorian literature: Modern essays in criticism,* edited by Austin Wright. Oxford: Oxford University Press.

Roy, Ashish. 1993. The fabulous imperialist semiotic of Wilkie Collins's *"The moonstone." New Literary History* 24, 3 (Summer): 657–81.

Roy, Parama. 1998. *Indian traffic.* Berkeley: University of California Press.

Said, Edward. 1979. *Orientalism.* New York: Vintage Books.

———. 1989. Introduction to *Kim,* by Rudyard Kipling. New York: Penguin.

———. 1993. *Culture and imperialism.* New York: Knopf.

Sayers, Dorothy. 1974. The omnibus of crime. In *Detective fiction: Crime and compromise,* edited by Dick Allen and David Chacko, 351–83. New York: Harcourt Brace Jovanovich.

Scheuermann, Mona. 1985. *Social protesting the eighteenth-century English novel.* Columbus: Ohio State University Press.

Schmitt, Cannon. 1997. *Alien nation: Nineteenth-century gothic fictions and English nationality.* Philadelphia: University of Pennsylvania Press.

Seeley, J. R. *The expansion of England.* Boston: Roberts Brothers, 1883.

Simmons, James C. 1971. Philip Meadows Taylor and the Anglo-Indian novel with a check list of his writings. *Bulletin of the New York Public Library* 75: 154–62.

Sleeman, James L. 1933. *Thug or a million murders.* London: Sampson Low, Marston.

Sleeman, William. 1836. *Ramaseeana.* 2 vols. Calcutta.

———. 1839. *The Thugs or Phansigars of India: comprising a history of the rise and progress of that extraordinary fraternity of assassins; and a description of the system which it pursues, and of the measures which have been adopted by the supreme government of India for its suppression.* Philadelphia: Carey and Hart.

———. 1844. *Rambles and recollections of an Indian official.* 2 vols. London: J. Hatchard.

Smiles, Samuel. 1870. The police of London. *The Quarterly Review* 129, 257 (July–October): 87–129.

Smith, Philip Thurmond. 1985. *Policing Victorian London: Political policing, public order, and the London Metropolitan Police.* Westport, CT: Greenwood Press.

Spry, Henry. 1837. *Modern India.*

Stallybrass, Peter, and Allon White. 1986. *The politics and poetics of transgression.* Ithaca: Cornell University Press.

Stanley, Henry Morton. 1895. *How I found Livingstone, travels, adventures, and discoveries in Central Africa, including four months' residence with Dr. Livingstone.* London: Sampson Low, Marston.

Stead, Philip John. 1985. *The police of Britain.* New York: Macmillan.

Stephen, Leslie. 1968. *The English utilitarians.* 3 vols. New York: Augustus M. Kelley.

Stocking, George W. 1987. *Victorian anthropology.* New York: The Free Press.

Stokes, Eric. 1959. *The English utilitarians and India.* Oxford: The Clarendon Press.

———. 1960. Macaulay: The Indian years. *A Review of English Literature* 1, 4 (October): 41–50.

Stone, Harry, ed. 1968. *Charles Dickens's uncollected writings from* Household Words, *1850–1859.* Bloomington: Indiana University Press.

Storch, Robert D. 1975. The plague of the blue locusts: Police reform and popular resistance in Northern England, 1840–1857. *International Review of Social History* 20, 1: 61–90.

Storch, Rudolph. 1967. Metaphors of private guilt and social rebellion in Godwin's *"Caleb Williams." ELH* 34, 2 (June): 188–207.

Suleri, Sara. 1992. *The rhetoric of English India.* Chicago: University of Chicago Press.

Symons, Julian. 1985. *Bloody murder: From the detective story to the crime novel: A history.* New York: Viking.

Tambling, Jeremy. 1995. *Dickens, violence and the modern state: Dreams of the scaffold.* New York: St. Martin's.

Taylor, Jenny Bourne. 1988. *In the secret theatre of home: Wilkie Collins, sensation narrative, and nineteenth-century psychology.* New York: Routledge.

Taylor, Philip Meadows. 1986. *Story of my life.* New Delhi: Asian Educational Services.

———. 1988. *Confessions of a Thug.* New Delhi: Asian Educational Services.

Thomas, Nicholas. 1994. *Colonialism's culture: Anthropology, travel and government.* Princeton: Princeton University Press.

Thomas, Ronald R. 1993. Minding the body politic: The romance of science and the revision of history in Victorian detective fiction. In *Victorian literature and culture,* vol. 19, 233–54. New York: AMS Press.

———. 1994. The fingerprint of the foreigner: Colonizing the criminal body in 1890s detective fiction and criminal anthropology. *ELH* 61: 655–83.

———. 1997. Double exposures: Arresting images in *"Bleak house"* and *"The house of the seven gables." Novel* 31, 1 (Fall): 87–113.

Thompson, E. P. 1966. *The makings of the English working class.* New York: Vintage.

———. 1975. *Whigs and hunters: The origin of the Black Act.* New York: Pantheon.

Thompson, Jon. 1993. *Fiction, crime, and empire.* Chicago: University of Illinois Press.

Thornton, Edward. 1837. *Illustrations of the history and practices of the Thugs: And notices of some of the proceedings of the government of India, for the suppression of the crime of thuggee.* London: W. H. Allen.

Trevelyan, Charles E. 1837. The Thugs; or, secret murderers of India. *Edinburgh Review* 64 (January): 357–95.

Trodd, Anthea. 1991. Introduction to *The moonstone,* by Wilkie Collins. New York: Oxford University Press.

Trumpener, Katie. 1997. *Bardic nationalism: The romantic novel and the British empire.* Princeton: Princeton University Press.

Tuker, Sir Francis. 1961. *The yellow scarf: The story of the life of Thuggee Sleeman.* London: Dent.

Wade, John. 1972 [1829]. *A treatise on the police and crimes of the metropolis.* Reprint Montclair, NJ: Patterson Smith.

Walker, Ronald, and June Frazer, eds. 1990. *The cunning craft: Original essays on detective fiction and contemporary literary theory.* Macomb, IL: Yeast Printing.

Ward, John. 1838. Police of the metropolis. *Edinburgh Review* 66 (January): 358–94.

Warren, Sir Charles. 1888. The police of the metropolis. *Murray's Magazine* 4 (November): 577–94.

White, Hayden. 1978. *Tropics of discourse: Essays in cultural criticism.* Baltimore: Johns Hopkins University Press.

_____. 1987. *The concept of the form: Narrative discourse and historical representation.* Baltimore: Johns Hopkins University Press.

Williams, Robert Grant. 1992–1993. Shadows of imperialism: Canonical typology in Taylor's *"Confessions of a Thug." Dalhousie Review* 72, 4 (Winter): 482–93.

Wilson, Edmund. 1970. *The wound and the bow.* New York: Oxford University Press.

Wiltse, Ed. 1998. "So constant an expectation": Sherlock Holmes and seriality. *Narrative* 6, 2 (May): 105–22.

Winks, Robin, ed. 1988. *Detective fiction: A collection of critical essays.* Woodstock, VT: Foul Play Press.

Woerkens, Martine van. 2002. *The strangled traveler: Colonial imaginings and the Thugs of India.* Translated by Catherine Tihanyi. Chicago: University of Chicago Press.

Wolfreys, Julian. 1994. *Being English: Narratives, idioms, and performances of national identity from Coleridge to Trollope.* Albany: State University of New York Press.

Woods, Robin. 1990. "His appearance is against him": The emergence of the detective. In *The cunning craft: Original essays on detective fiction and contemporary literary theory,* edited by Ronald Walker and June Frazer, 15–23. Macomb, IL: Yeast Printing.

Wreford, Henry G. . 1850. Spy police. *Household Words* (September 21): 611–14.

Wright, Caleb. 1849. *Lectures on India: Also, descriptions of remarkable customs and personages in other pagan and Mohammedan countries.* Boston: Caleb Wright.

Wynter, Andrew. 1856. The police and the thieves. *The Quarterly Review* (June): 160–96.

Yang, Anand, ed. 1985. *Crime and criminality in British India.* Tucson: University of Arizona Press.

Yeats-Brown, F. 1938a. Biographical sketch of Meadows Taylor. In *Confessions of a Thug,* edited by F. Yeats-Brown, 1–44. London: Eyre & Sottiswoode.

——. 1938b. Introduction to *Confessions of a Thug.* Edited by F. Yeats-Brown. London: Eyre & Sottiswoode.

Young, G. M. 1967. *Victorian England: Portrait of an age.* New York: Oxford University Press.

INDEX

"The Adventure of the Bruce
  Partington Plans" (Doyle), 68–69,
  71
Anderson, Benedict, xv, 91n. 10
Anderson, David, and David
  Killingray, 91n. 10, 93n. 20, 98n.
  15
Auden, W. H., 67

Baucom, Ian, xix, 91n. 10
Bentham, Jeremy/Benthamism, xxi, 3,
  30, 91n. 9, 96n. 9
Bhabha, Homi, 91n. 10
Bleak House (Dickens), xvi–xvii, 22,
  47, 53–54, 86, 100n. 1, 102n. 20
Bloody Code, the, 2, 40
Brantlinger, Patrick, 37, 76, 93n. 26,
  97n. 3, 99n. 18, 101n. 12, 107n.
  23
Brogden, Mike, 23, 91n. 10, 93n. 20,
  94n. 2
Buchan, John, 81–85. See also *The
  Thirty-Nine Steps*
Bulwer Lytton, Sir Edward, 35
Burke, Edmund, xiii, 3, 79, 90n. 6
Butler, Judith, xviii
Butler, Marilyn, 10, 94n. 3

Caleb Williams (Godwin), xvi, 1–11,
  13, 16, 21, 56, 67–68, 82, 86,
  94n. 3
Cannadine, David, 80, 107nn. 1–2
Cawelti, John, xv, 60, 100nn. 6–7
Chadwick, Edwin, 19, 90n. 3, 91n. 9
  96n. 9
Clifford, James, 99n. 22
Colley, Linda, 58, 91n. 10, 94n. 1,
  101 nn. 13, 15

Collins, Philip, 45, 49, 99n. 25
Collins, Wilkie, xxv, 6, 43–46, 49,
  55–63, 83–84, 102nn. 20–22,
  102n. 29, 103n. 30. See also *The
  Moonstone*
Colquhoun, Patrick, 18, 90n. 5, 93n.
  27
Confessions of a Thug (Taylor), 22,
  25–27, 35, 37–42, 56, 93n. 26,
  96n. 1, 105n. 7
Critchley, T. A., 1, 9, 19
curiosity, 6, 9, 14, 26–29, 41–42, 61,
  83

David, Dierdre, 36–37, 97n. 3, 99n.
  18, 101n. 11, 102nn. 24, 26,
  103n. 32
Davis, Nuel Pharr, 102n. 22
Deconstruction, xviii
detection, as a methodology, xiv–xvii,
  xxii–xxiii, 2, 4, 8–10, 14, 16, 23,
  27–28, 41, 47, 52,–53, 57–61, 65,
  67–68, 71, 74, 79, 81–86, 104n.
  6, 105n. 7; the Detection Club, xv,
  67, 91n. 11
detective: and credibility, 21, 24,
  31–32, 67; and criminality, 11; the
  Detective Police, 29, 44, 90n. 3,
  100n. 2; figure of the, xiii–xxv, 2,
  4, 8–11, 15, 20, 22–24, 30,
  32–35, 40, 42, 45–63, 65, 67,
  70–75, 77–87, 89n.3, 93n. 24,
  94n. 28, 98n. 11, 99n. 19, 102n.
  29, 103n. 1, 106n. 17; and France,
  1, 44, 51, 83, 94n. 1; and intelligence, 22–23, 27–29, 79, 97n. 9;
  and liberalism, xxi, 23–24, 53, 67,
  101n. 16; and self–defense, 9,

119